PER PHRASES

for

LETTERS OF RECOMMENDATION

**Hundreds of Ready-to-Use Phrases
You Can Use to Recommend
Applicants to College, Grad School,
and Professional School**

Paul Bodine

New York Chicago San Francisco Lisbon London Madrid Mexico City
Milan New Delhi San Juan Seoul Singapore Sydney Toronto

Library of Congress Cataloging-in-Publication Data

Bodine, Paul, 1959–.
    Perfect phrases for letters of recommendation / by Paul Bodine.
        p.   cm.
    ISBN-13: 978-0-07-162654-5
    ISBN-10: 0-07-162654-9
    1. Employment references.   2. Universities and colleges—Admission.
 3. Letter writing.   4. Exposition (Rhetoric).   5. Business writing.   I. Title.

    HF5549.5.R45 B63   2010
    651.7'5—dc22   2009045529

1 2 3 4 5 6 7 8 9 10 11 12 13 14 15 16 17 18 19 20 21 22   DOC/DOC   0 9

ISBN   978-0-07-162654-5
MHID   0-07-162654-9

Note: All the examples used in this book are fictional. The names of actual organizations have been used only for illustrative purposes and are not intended to represent or characterize the actual organizations.

For Tamami, again.

Contents

Contents

Part 3   The Core Strengths

Contents

Part 4   Other Strengths and Weaknesses

Contents

Part 5   Concluding Sections

Preface

For many professionals, whether educators or businesspeople, writing recommendation letters for applicants to college, professional school, or graduate school is an unpleasant and time-consuming process—even for the vast majority who are eager to help their applicants and have good things to say. Everyone is pressed for time, and sometimes the right words just don't come. This book is intended to ease the would-be recommender's burden by providing extended examples of effective praise for a wide variety of the most common recommendation letter topics.

As a professional admissions consultant for applicants to college and professional and graduate schools since 1997, I've reviewed hundreds of recommendation letters from every kind of recommender. I've seen what works and what doesn't. The product of that experience is this book's examples, "perfect phrases" that incorporate the kind of recommendation content that I've seen work with the admissions committees of the world's best universities. This book is divided into the following sections:

Part 1, "Writing Letters of Recommendation," discusses the basics of writing recommendation letters, from typical letter topics to the importance of using examples.

Part 2, "The Preliminaries," covers such typical letter sections as the introduction, the recommender's relationship with the applicant, the applicant's rank, and the applicant's career progress.

In Part 3, "The Core Strengths," such common recommendation topics as leadership, teamwork, intellectual and professional ability, and communication skills are illustrated with examples from letters for college, graduate school, and professional school applicants.

Part 4, "Other Strengths and Weaknesses," provides examples for other common letter topics like multicultural or international skills, character and integrity, volunteering and social impact activities, and initiative and creativity.

Finally, in Part 5, "Concluding Sections," examples are provided for the goals and potential sections, letter sections on specific degrees (e.g., the M.B.A., J.D., M.D., etc.), and the closing phrases of your recommendation letter.

Note that the topics illustrated in this book are not "pure" categories. The traits that make an applicant a good leader are often the same as those that make her a good team player, so describing an applicant's leadership prowess may involve referring explicitly to teamwork skills. Similarly, it's perfectly acceptable for a recommender to describe an applicant's career progress and simultaneously rank the applicant against her peers. Or a recommender may comment on an applicant's integrity while responding to a recommendation question about volunteer activities. The point is this: the strengths that make an applicant appealing to schools are often interrelated and self-reinforcing. Moreover, an effective recommender often maximizes the limited space provided by communicating as much positive information and touching on as many themes as possible. For all these reasons, the reader will find that many of the examples in this book illustrate multiple overlapping strengths.

Some readers may wonder why a book of "perfect phrases" is full of paragraphs. The answer is that no matter how well crafted it is, praise alone will not get your applicant accepted. Examples— extended, meaty, concrete examples—substantiating that praise will. Of course, you *will* find a wealth of ready-to-use phrases of enthusiastic support in this book, but when you do you will always see them attached to the detailed examples that make them real and credible.

Though this book is addressed to recommenders, applicants may benefit from it in two ways: in understanding what makes recommendation letters work and in better preparing themselves to help their recommenders write the best letters they possibly can.

The author welcomes any comments or inquiries on the content of this book; e-mail me at paulbodine@live.com.

Part 1

Writing Letters of Recommendation

Chapter 1

Convincing Praise, Credible Enthusiasm

Whether your applicant is applying to college, professional school, or graduate school, letters of recommendation will play a critical role in his or her admissions success. The recommendation letter has a special power because it is the only element in the admissions folder in which a third party other than the applicant and the school is given the chance to weigh in on the applicant's qualifications. A detailed, enthusiastic, and well-written recommendation that corroborates the message conveyed by the applicant's essays and application can lend the applicant an air of credibility that's hard to beat. This is especially true for schools, like many law schools, that don't interview applicants: the recommendation letter enables the admissions committee to gain a unique perspective on the applicant's profile. For an applicant who lies in the middle of his target schools' application pool—where a hairbreadth difference separates one candidate from the next—the impact of recommendation letters on admission decisions can be enormous.

Why do schools give such weight to documents that are almost always dripping with praise? While it's true that the majority of letters are positive, a significant number of recommendations are overtly negative or largely positive but loaded with enough hints of darker truths about the applicant to push her into the reject pile. More importantly, a much larger percentage of letters are so vague, brief, poorly written, or obviously penned by the applicant that their value to the admissions committee is nil. It's because of this general lack of quality and reliability that a detailed, well-written letter of recommendation can mean so much to your applicant's chances.

Recommendation Letters: Content and What You Should Expect from Your Applicant

Though a medical school is obviously looking for different skills than a graduate program in English literature, all good recommendation letters tell schools whether the applicant can handle its program academically and whether he has the potential to succeed professionally. All good recommendation letters will inform schools about the applicant's hard (technical, analytical, or scholarly) skills and soft (interpersonal, communication, writing) skills. Finally, all effective letters will tell the school something about the applicant's personality and character.

This book is divided into the topics recommenders are most commonly asked to comment on:

- Growth and career progress (Chapter 5)
- Leadership skills (Chapter 6)
- Interpersonal and teamwork skills (Chapter 7)
- Analytical, academic, and professional skills (Chapter 8)
- Writing and communication skills (Chapter 9)
- Multicultural and international skills (Chapter 10)
- Character and integrity (Chapter 11)
- Volunteering and social impact (Chapter 12)
- Initiative and creativity (Chapter 13)
- Weaknesses (Chapter 14)
- Goals and potential (Chapter 15)

Which of these topics your applicant will ask you to comment on will depend on the type of school she is applying to (e.g., graduate, professional, or college) and the specific recommendation requirements of the schools she is targeting. Given the broad range of these topics, it can be daunting (particularly for professionals new to writing recommendations) to figure out where to start and what exactly to say about your applicant. That's where your applicant should lend you a hand. Expect him to provide you with the following:

- A résumé or curriculum vitae
- The schools' specific recommendation questions and instructions for submitting the finished letter
- Academic transcripts (for applicants in college or recently graduated from college)

- For educators: A list of the classes she took with you, together with the grades she earned and one or two of her tests or papers from those classes
- For educators: Highlights of and/or your comments on the applicant's classroom work
- For employers: Your periodic performance reviews of the applicant
- A general statement explaining postdegree goals, what the applicant thinks is unique and compelling about his candidacy (traits, not just skills), and even specific stories you might use to answer each of the schools' specific questions

If your applicant only gives you a résumé and a parting "good luck," then you need to educate him on his responsibilities. It goes without saying that an applicant should give you not just a couple of weeks but hopefully a month or two to write the letter. If he doesn't, cry foul.

Ideally, your applicant will tell you what other types of recommenders (e.g., employers, professors, volunteer activity supervisors, etc.) she is requesting letters from, and what themes or stories she doesn't need you to comment on (since another recommender will). Your applicant should have selected her recommenders so the broadest range of her skills, experiences, and themes are being communicated to the schools. This breadth will minimize the potential overlap between the stories each recommender tells. Of course, it's no disaster if you and another recommender refer to one or two of the same stories, as long as you provide a fresh perspective on them. Moreover, common recommendation topics like "leadership" and "teamwork" are so broad that multiple recommenders should be able to provide original slants on each theme without repetition. The bottom line: it will help you in writing a good letter to know your applicant's total recommendation strategy, including what aspects of his profile you should address—but it is the applicant's responsibility to provide this information to you.

Examples: The Heart of the Recommendation Letter

Ask admissions officials at whatever level what they value most in a recommendation letter, and you'll probably hear two words: *candor* and *examples*. They want to know that you are being honest with them and that your praise is backed up by objective facts, concrete examples.

The majority of recommenders dole out effusive praise in generous heaps, but because they don't support their enthusiasm with specific examples, the admissions committee (adcom) is left to assume that recommenders mean well but can't really support their assertions. Some schools refer to these kinds of letters (when they come from professors) as DWIC ("did well in class") letters; they tell the school nothing.

As a rule of thumb, follow every sentence of praise ("Alex's research skills are spectacular") with several sentences that illustrate this praise. The illustrative wording can be a single extended example or multiple short examples. If your example is extended, the following three-part structure may help you present it effectively:

1. What was the problem or challenge that the applicant or the applicant's organization faced? (For example, "Alex chose to write a paper proving that Stephen Douglas should have won the 1860 election.")

2. How did the applicant use the particular skill in question (in this case, research skills) to resolve this problem or challenge? That is, what steps did he take in applying this skill and overcoming the specific obstacles he faced? ("Alex not only reviewed key secondary sources but primary sources as well. I was quite impressed when he requested and gained permission to examine Douglas's personal papers at the University of Illinois. Two letters he discovered showed that Douglas himself believed that two tactical blunders had cost him the election.")

3. What was the positive outcome (expressed quantitatively, if possible)? ("I gave Alex an A and recommended him for departmental honors.")

Back up each of your claims with examples, and, if you can, back up your examples with concrete numbers ("Doris's proposal led to productivity gains of 4 percent, representing $500,000 in labor cost savings"). Examples and details are the payload, the lifeblood, of the recommendation letter—proof that you aren't just blowing laudatory smoke rings. Without them, your letter will become instantly forgettable. With enough of them, the admissions reader's skepticism will gradually be converted into belief and, ideally, growing enthusiasm.

In addition to examples, you may also occasionally need to provide the context for understanding them. In other words, you shouldn't just state that the applicant presented his market analysis to the CEO, if you could also add that only one other associate has ever done that in the history of the firm. Frame your examples so readers perceive their significance in the way you want them to.

Strategic Considerations

The savviest recommenders—usually those with the deepest experience writing letters, such as educators and management consultants—will do more than provide credible enthusiasm. They will also understand each applicant's particular challenges and do damage control to offset them. Your applicant should tell you if his application carries red flags like low grades, weak extracurriculars, or lack of leadership. Even if he doesn't tell you, you'll be doing your best for him if you compensate for these weaknesses by citing offsetting evidence. For example: "Tom's grades were not in his class's top third, but they do show a powerful upward trend (his senior-year GPA was 3.7), and he worked 20 hours a week all four years."

Many applicants' challenges are not weaknesses at all, just "perception problems": the applicant belongs to an applicant pool that invites certain natural assumptions by admissions officers—the quantitatively challenged sales rep, the interpersonally unpolished technical student, the investment banker without a social conscience. Help your applicant fight these assumptions with examples that work against the typecasting. For an applicant who has no experience overseas, for example, you could discuss the details of her successful interaction on a team staffed with multinational professionals.

Length

Your applicant will tell you how long your letter should be. As a general rule, however, you should jettison any idea that a good recommendation letter is a page in length. That may once have been the case, but—again, generally speaking—the more selective the school your applicant is targeting, the more space you should feel free to take in enthusing about his qualities. As long as your letter is meaty, two and even three or more single-spaced pages is a perfectly valid length for an applicant who has many virtues to sing. Law schools, for example, generally do not place length restrictions on recommendation letters because they want recommenders to feel encouraged to say as much as they choose to. A one-page letter may send the unintended signal that you don't really have much to say about the applicant; a four-pager, however, may try the patience of an admissions officer buried under hundreds of applicant files.

Asking the Applicant to Write It

More and more recommenders are asking applicants to draft their recommendation letters for them. If you want to help your applicant get admitted, you should not be one of them. Schools' purposes in asking a third party—you—to provide outside perspective on the applicant's potential are defeated if that "outside" perspective comes directly from the applicant. Asking the applicant to write the recommendation for you usually produces a very mediocre letter. An applicant is unlikely to be able to view himself the way a more experienced, more objective individual can. And even the most egotistical applicant will probably not be able to describe himself with the same delighted, spontaneous enthusiasm that a truly supportive recommender can generate.

Moreover, given that admissions officers read thousands of recommendation letters over their careers, they develop a sixth sense for nongenuine letters. After plowing through the applicant's essays, the admissions officers are likely to be aware of his stylistic idiosyncrasies and able to detect them quickly in a ventriloquized letter.

If you really can't write the letter yourself, gently tell the applicant to find another recommender who will. Don't worry that you'll be hurting her feelings; you'll actually be doing her a favor. Too many recommenders grudgingly agree to write letters but then, regretting their generosity, submit tepid, short, or vague letters that do more harm than good. If you really can't (or don't want to) write the letter yourself, recuse yourself.

If, on the other hand, you really do want to write a letter for the applicant but are truly pressed for time, consider an option that will minimize your time and keep the applicant out of the process, as the schools prefer. As an experienced admissions consultant, the author can interview you, record your responses to the school's recommendation questions, and transcribe and edit them into a letter draft that you can then revise or sign. This removes the applicant from the process and enables you to juggle your enthusiasm for the applicant with your busy schedule. E-mail the author at paul bodine@live.com for details.

Part 2

The Preliminaries

Chapter 2

Perfect Phrases for Introductions

Though schools are increasingly asking recommenders to submit their letters online, traditional paper-based letters follow the format and conventional courtesies of a standard business letter, including a brief general introduction: "It's my distinct pleasure to write this letter of recommendation on behalf of . . ." Though such positive language can help establish a tone of enthusiasm, it can also sound canned, so—if your letter will have an introduction—feel free to open creatively, in any way that will catch the admissions reader's attention and help your applicant stand out. Whether it's an anecdote about the first time you met the applicant or a summary of the key qualities that make the applicant unique, your introduction can begin establishing that you know your applicant well and have good reasons for recommending him.

The introduction is also a good place for you to provide a few sentences of background information on yourself—where you earned your degree(s) and which organizations you've worked for and in what capacity, up to your present title. Such information can enhance your credibility as someone whose opinion of the applicant merits attention. If you have the degree your applicant seeks, you should note this, especially if you earned it at the school the applicant is targeting. The more impressive your bio is, the more space you may want to give it (if space permits).

Which credentials you should highlight will depend on the kind of degree your applicant wants to pursue. For example, if your applicant is applying to a scholarly graduate program and you are an academic, then you should highlight your own credentials as a scholar (e.g., where have your papers been published?). If your applicant is applying to business school and you are a manager, then you should underscore your graduate management education (if you have an M.B.A.) and mention your career pace and responsibilities as a manager. If your applicant is applying to college and you are a high school teacher or advisor, you should highlight your years of experience teaching or advising high schoolers.

After providing some perfect phrases for opening your letter, we follow with perfect phrases about the recommenders' background, grouped into the following three recommender types: academic recommenders; employers; and community-related, extracurricular, and other recommenders.

Perfect Phrases for Introductions

- I am very pleased to have this opportunity to warmly recommend Mr. James Anderson for admission to the University of Texas at Austin. He is an outstanding person and a student of exceptional promise who can contribute substantially to your program.

- Last year, 26 Nebraska students asked me to write recommendation letters for them. For some, I encouraged them to consider other professors. For many, I did my best to study the materials they provided so I'd remember them clearly enough to help them. For only three did I sit down to the task with the relish I bring to this letter for Donald Green.

- In my capacity as Mary Thompson's direct supervisor at Wal-Mart and as a Columbia M.B.A. who has interacted with multiple Wharton alumni over my 20-year career, I strongly believe Mary is a uniquely compelling candidate for your M.B.A. program.

- Let me tell you about Sandra Reed.

- I didn't hesitate to agree to write this letter on behalf of Maria Garcia's application to the University of Illinois. I believe her academic potential is very strong but, more than that, through her leadership at Santa Ysabel High School she has proved herself to be a person of character who deserves the quality education your program provides.

- Thank you for this opportunity to express my admiration for the intellectual gifts, public spiritedness, and professional potential of Mr. Deepak Tuli.

- Maturity, strategic vision, formidable analytical skills, the proverbial heart of gold—if I didn't know Kent Barset personally, I might think him to good to be true. Please don't make that mistake.

- I am pleased and honored to recommend Jeffery Cook for the Class of 2012 at the Yale School of Management. As an SOM alumna, I believe that Jeffery will be a tremendous addition to the Yale community, enriching the experience of his classmates and effectively representing both Yale and SOM as he pursues his business career.

- Over the past 20 months, Ms. Annie Le has come to my attention as an exceptionally able and talented law clerk and paralegal, an extraordinarily engaged researcher, and a very diligent and reliable employee with an outstanding command of the English language.

- As the cofounder of Priscilla's House, Inc., and President of FashionNation USA, I work with many talented individuals who are excellent at breakthrough creative design and the implementation of game-changing marketing campaigns. Management in this type of environment requires diverse skill sets, including the ability to communicate to multiple audiences—internal creative teams, account management teams, and clients. Roger Bravotti is one of those unique individuals who is capable of operating effectively in a fast-paced, competitive, and dynamic environment without losing his cool or his class. For this reason, I am honored to write this letter on his behalf.

- This letter represents my very strong and sincere endorsement of Rebecca Carter, a young person of great promise in Galveston's literary community.

- I can still vividly recall the first day I met Ms. Eileen Turner.

• I welcome this opportunity to recommend Peter Joss to your master's program. As a colleague of his at First Financial, I have repeatedly witnessed Pete's raw finance skills, his ability to inspire people, and the sheer energy and conviction he brings to the pursuit of his goals.

• During the three years in which I have known Anna Morris, I have had the pleasure of working with her in both academic and extracurricular settings. I have watched her grow as a student and as a person. She is an individual I take genuine pleasure in recommending.

• This letter is written to offer my vigorous endorsement of Laura Morgan's application for admission to University of Michigan Law School. I believe Ms. Morgan will be an outstanding contributor to the Law School and the larger university community, and I urge you give her application your closest consideration.

• Last January, I learned from Carol Beemer's premed advisor that she had decided to apply for admission to Johns Hopkins School of Medicine. Before waiting for her to ask, I offered to write her a letter of recommendation. I've done that on only one previous occasion, for Joe Sanchez (JHU M.D. '07), who is now doing his residency at St. Vincent's Hospital in Manhattan.

• As soon as I finished reading Brenda Moore's senior thesis, "Corporate Punishment in Australian Private Schools," I thought of the University of Minnesota. As my student in two classes and my thesis advisee, Brenda combines a passion for teaching and research that your interdisciplinary Master in Education program can nurture for the benefit of future students who are fortunate enough to have her as a teacher.

- Having hired two Haas M.B.A.s and worked alongside four others, I am acutely aware of the school's high standards, spirit of innovation, and sense of social purpose. It's because of this personal knowledge that I write to strongly recommend Mr. Szeyuan Yun for admission to the Haas School of Business. He is an outstanding young manager with extraordinary potential.

- It's been my privilege to teach Ross Blitzbaum for two years now. I can think of few other students more likely to benefit from the innovative, rigorous, and intimate learning community of Reed College.

- Donna Washington is an unforgettable and dynamic individual with the intellectual tools, language skills, and drive and clear purpose to succeed at Stanford Law School.

- Having recommended eight Duke Law J.D.s to you from my institution, I think I can say I understand the kind of person who will thrive in your program. I have never recommended anyone whom I did not believe could truly excel at Duke Law. For the reasons I enumerate below, Ruth Lopez will certainly thrive in Durham.

- Mark Fofana is one of the brightest, most dedicated, and impressive individuals I know, and I recommend him to the Washington University School of Medicine as a student of unusually strong potential.

- My dear colleague and friend, Kevin Lee, has informed me of his intention to apply to Insead's M.B.A. program, and because I consider him a unique and exceptional candidate I am happy to support him.

Perfect Phrases for Recommender's Background

Educators or Academics

- I earned my B.S. in Electrical Engineering at McMaster University in Ontario and my M.A. in Education at California State University Northridge in 1997. I began teaching math and science at San Jacinto High School that same year, and in 1998 became assistant coach on San Jacinto's varsity basketball team. I have been serving as a student advisor/counselor since the fall of 2003.

- I earned my bachelor's degree in education at the University of Michigan in 1987, my master's in education at the University of Oregon in 1989, and my doctorate in education here at University of Washington (UW) in 1993. After becoming Associate Professor of Education, Curriculum, and Instruction in UW's Education department, I joined UW's Tacoma Education Center (an off-campus graduate center), where I currently serve as director. I teach four courses in the areas of multicultural education and ethnic studies. I have published a textbook, *Rainbow Learning: A Methodology*, and numerous articles in *Educational Review* and *Teaching Education*.

• After graduating 10th in my class at the U.S. Naval Academy in Annapolis, I served for 10 years as a naval officer aboard the USS *Abraham Lincoln*. In 1993, I earned my master's degree in biotechnology from Penn State and then served as the assistant academic dean there for five years before joining Loyola University as academic dean in 1998. I've been a member of Loyola's premed committee since 2003.

• After earning my B.A. in English at University of New Hampshire, I earned my Ph.D. in English at Leeds University in 1990. I served as Assistant and Associate Professor of English at Bradley University from 1991 to 2005. I am currently Associate Professor of English at Indiana University in Bloomington and a prelaw advisor since 2007. I also teach the undergraduate elective, "The Law in Literature." I have successfully recommended five of my students to your law school in the past four years.

• I graduated from Rice University in 1982 with a degree in chemical engineering and earned my Ph.D. in the same subject at University of New Mexico. I have been a member of the engineering faculty at University of Oklahoma since 1989. I have been Bridgeway Distinguished Professor of Engineering since 2001 and the director of graduate research since 2003. My published research focuses on anaerobic digestion of agricultural and food wastes and has appeared in such journals as *International Journal of Food Science & Technology* and *Industrial and Engineering Chemical Research*.

• I earned my bachelor's degree in math at Eastern Arkansas State University and my master's in education at Harding University. I have taught math and physical education at Burnside High School since 1992. I have earned certifications in math and physical education, and my current assignments (since 2002) are Algebra 2, Honors Algebra 2, and Honors Geometry. I've served as a student counselor since 2007.

Employers

• Before earning my M.B.A. at Tuck in 1995, I negotiated Chile's external debt with creditors like the International Monetary Fund (1990–91) and served on the special economic team of Chile's Finance Ministry. In 1994, Credit Suisse's Latin America Investment Banking Group hired me to manage mergers and acquisitions, project finance, and privatizations and to coordinate the activities of its Zurich and Chilean offices. After earning my Tuck M.B.A., I became managing director of the Latin America Investment Banking Group in 1997.

• With a Bachelor of Science in Electrical Engineering from Temple University, I joined the Patent and Trade Office as a Patent Examiner in 2000 and have risen to Senior Patent Examiner and then in 2006 to Supervising Patent Examiner. Today, I hire, train, and promote examiners and manage, review, and sign off on the work of the 15 patent examiners in my group, including Michelle.

• I have for worked for two Denny's Restaurants in northern New Jersey as a cook, waiter, and assistant manager since I was 16. I graduated from Essex County College's Food Service/Hospitality program in 2004 and became manager at the Denny's of Avenel, New Jersey, two years ago, where I hired and trained Thomas.

• I am currently the Chief Financial Officer of Speedway Performance Systems and worked with Eddie while I was a Vice President at UBS. By way of background, I spent the last 10 years in venture capital (CCMP Capital Advisors and TPG Capital) and, more recently, investment banking (UBS). I earned my M.B.A. at the University of Chicago in 1994.

• I am a partner with Crowell & Moring LLP's Tax Group. We are a prominent full-service law firm with more than 440 attorneys and offices in New York, Washington, California, London, and Brussels. I personally have practiced tax law for more than 20 years, earning my J.D. from New York University School of Law. I was named partner at Crowell & Moring in 2003 and have been head of the Tax Group in New York since 2006. I specialize in the domestic and international tax aspects of business and financial transactions, including mergers and acquisitions, reorganizations, joint ventures, and cross-border tax planning.

• Prior to obtaining my Doctor of Dental Medicine degree, I had careers in both education and nursing, experiences that helped me realize that dentistry would be the most fulfilling career path for me. As a result, I attended dental school at University of Connecticut School of Dental Medicine, graduating at the age of 33. Since 2001, I have run a successful general practice in Grove Beach, a small town 25 miles north of New Haven.

Community-Related, Extracurricular, and Other Recommenders

• I am the executive director of the Apert Syndrome Foundation (ASF), which I started twenty years ago when my youngest son was born with that condition. Our mission is to raise public awareness about Apert Syndrome and to lend financial and emotional support to victims of the condition and their family members (please see asf.org for information). I personally interview and train all of our staff, including volunteers like Luke. Outside of ASF, I am a financial planner and advisor for Ameriprise Financial.

• I am a Master Sergeant with Expeditionary Strike Group Three, formerly Amphibious Group (COMPHIBGRU) Three, based out of San Diego, California. In my 16 years in the Marine Corps, I have served in every major service command and worked on each general staff. I served two tours of duty in Operation Iraqi Freedom.

• I am a native Cambodian who returned home to Phnom Penh 5 years ago after 10 years working as an interpreter in Hanoi, Beijing, and Tokyo. I now serve as the Team Leader for International Liaison with Kiva's Cambodia Field Office in Phnom Penh. A Royal University of Phnom Penh graduate in English, I have worked closely with M.B.A.s (including two Wharton M.B.A.s) both as an interpreter and in my NGO work.

• I earned a bachelor's degree in psychology at Colgate and a master's in divinity from Union Theological Seminary before earning my doctorate in theology from the Colorado Theological Seminary in 1998. I became Senior Pastor at Trinity Church in 2006 after eight years as Assistant Pastor at Wichita Church of Christ. I started the Trinity Cares Outreach program, which Jonathan now leads, in 2007.

• After earning my J.D. from Georgetown Law Center, I joined Representative Meg Dunphy's office as a legislative aide and ultimately rose to chief of staff. When Representative Dunphy retired, I became chief of staff for Representative Mavis Ordman, focusing primarily on her duties for the Labor, Health, and Human Services Subcommittee. In 2007, I began supervising interns like Chip.

• I joined the girls' lacrosse coaching staff at Middletown High School in the fall of 2001 and am now in my ninth season as the Junior Varsity coach. After graduating from Middletown myself, I earned my Bachelor of Science from Loyola College in 1997 with a double major in physical education and sports therapy. I helped establish a women's lacrosse program at Calvert Hills High School in 1998 before returning to Middletown as a coach in 2001.

Chapter 3

Perfect Phrases for Recommender's Relationship with the Applicant

Most schools explicitly ask recommenders to describe how long they've known the applicant and in what context. On the most general level, this question establishes that you know the applicant well enough to have useful comments to make about him. In some contexts, this "relationship" question helps the schools ensure that the applicant is providing letters from the required mix of recommenders. For example, some medical schools ask for recommendation letters from both science faculty and nonscience faculty, and your answer to the relationship question clarifies which category you belong to.

If you can convincingly establish that you have extensive and sustained knowledge of the applicant, you will create a climate of credibility that will make all your later assertions about him more believable. (Conversely, if your relationship with the applicant is not as close or as long-standing, you may want to keep this section of the letter short and sweet—or tell the applicant to find another recommender.)

If you are an employer writing a letter for an applicant who worked for you, try to answer the following questions in this section of the letter:

- How did you first get to know the applicant? Did you hire her?
- What were the applicant's responsibilities when she first began working with you?
- What, early on, was your hierarchical relationship with the applicant? Did she report directly to you?
- How often did you meet, talk, or interact with the applicant? Continually (your offices or cubicles were side by side, for example) or intermittently—twice a day, once a week? If the latter, did you only meet formally in meetings, for example? If so, were these group or one-on-one meetings?
- How has the applicant's responsibilities changed over time? Has your hierarchical reporting relationship with her changed over the duration of your relationship?
- How has the context or frequency of your interaction with the applicant changed over time? If you no longer work together, when did you last work with her and how often do you keep in touch?

If you are an academic or educator writing a letter for a student, try to answer the following questions:

- What were the specific courses or settings in which you first came to know the applicant? Were you a teaching assistant in a tutorial or small seminar? Were you a professor teaching a large lecture class or a graduate-level seminar that allowed undergraduates to enroll?
- What were the difficulty levels of these courses, and what was your grading policy in these courses? How often did these classes meet, and how many students were enrolled? What textbooks did you use? How many papers or tests did you assign?
- In what ways did the applicant first stand out from other students, and how (if at all) did he build a deeper relationship with you over time?
- How often did you meet or talk with the applicant?
- Did you have opportunities to get to know the applicant outside of class? If so, detail the nature and extent of that interaction.
- Did the applicant do any extended project, research, or thesis work for you?
- If the applicant has graduated, how has he sustained the relationship?

Now let's take a look at perfect phrases describing academic, employment, extracurricular, and peer recommenders' relationships with the applicant.

Perfect Phrases for Academic Recommenders

• I first met Judi in 2007 when she enrolled in Wichita State's master's program in education. She took my 20-student pedagogical methods class in the fall semester of 2007. I found her class comments to be relevant and thoughtful and consistently helpful in reorienting a wayward discussion or nudging a stale one down a fresh path. In addition to teaching her, I have followed her progress throughout the program in my role as the Academic Director of the Education program, meeting with her once a month in this capacity. In 2008, I became Judi's advisor on her Senior Thesis Project, which entailed supervising her work in two project classes over eight months. For her thesis, Judi researched and wrote a study investigating the effects of external environmental noise on knowledge retention. During this period, I met with her twice weekly and exchanged e-mails with her, sometimes daily. Usually, at the middle or near the end of the master's program, the class and I have a small get-together or party to socialize. With these activities, I can get to know students on a personal level, understand their academic and professional concerns, and help address those concerns. Some of these students become my friends. I met Judi outside of class socially in this way, at department parties, and even met her parents on one occasion. Because of this extended and intensive interaction, I have come to know Judi well.

• I am the Sterling Professor Emeritus of History at Oklahoma State University and chair of the university's history department. I have taught at the university for over 20 years. I teach a historiographic methods class open to undergraduates and graduate-level seminars (open to select undergraduates) in Native American history, problems in North American colonialism, and the history of the Southwest United States. I was in the fortunate position of being able to teach Gary Korman in all four of these classes over the past two years. He wrote more than 10 papers for me, was one of the four most active participants in my classes, and frequently took advantage of my office hours. In my role as advisor to the university's Native American Students Club, I also advised Gary when he established a speaker series and a film series. I believe I can comment on his intellectual gifts and potential contribution to the history profession with some insight.

• My first encounter with Abhinav was while teaching Mountain Valley High's two-year Spanish program. Born in India, Abhinav moved to the United States when he was young and immediately became fascinated by Mexican culture and the Spanish language. The only Indian student in the class, he not only stood out as an engaging, pleasant, and serious student, but his Spanish was already very advanced (he earned an "A" in all my classes). Outside of the classroom, I encourage my students to improve their Spanish skills by becoming community volunteers. Abhinav jumped at the opportunity. For the past two years now, he has volunteered part-time for Eureka Valley Hispanic Services (EVHS), a nonprofit agency where I served as a Client Advocate until October 2009. Because our interactions in class and at EVHS enable us to see each other as many as five times a week, Abhinav and I have gotten to know each other very well.

• In addition to her regular participation in my lecture course, Molecular Biology (in which she was among my five best students), Christine Davis worked under my direct supervision as one of four undergraduate research assistants in my lab from September 2007 to December 2009. We worked side by side up to 20 hours a week on research involving the development and function of olfactory neurons in *C. elegans*. Because she is a natural researcher, I tended to let her lead her lab mates, which meant I tended to interact with her more than others. Over the 16 months Christine studied and worked with me, she never missed a single class, lab session, or opportunity to meet with me during my office hours. I am therefore able to discuss the quality of her mind and the extent of her interests in much more detail than I can with most students I write letters for.

• Raymond Wolfe was my student in two classes at Spangler Preparatory: Engineering Technology and Advanced Placement Calculus. In both courses, he earned among the three highest grades I gave out. He was a very extroverted student in class, and he once asked if I needed his help getting a transfer student up to speed. He's the kind of student you remember. He was also very, very active in Spangler's decision to adopt Project Lead the Way (pltw.org), an innovative program that exposes high school kids to engineering, aeronautics, and other applied math and science fields through hands-on learning. Ray heard about it from a cousin on the East Coast and enlisted me and two other Spangler science teachers in pushing Spangler to try it out. I know Ray about as well as any student I've ever taught.

Perfect Phrases for Employers

• I have personally known Walter for nine years, ever since he joined Costco's Atlanta regional headquarters as a 20-hour-per-week student employee in the advertising department. Costco Southeast usually hires final-semester university students part-time in order to then offer a very limited number of them full-time employment upon completion of their studies, depending on their performance. Walter was somewhat special in that he joined the company with four semesters still to go at Emory. We had never done this before, given that we give our part-timers a heavy work-load. But Walter was eager, and under my supervision, he handled his dual duties so well that ever since then we've continued hiring students with up to four semesters left in college. Of course, I hired Walter as soon as he graduated, and working directly for me (multiple interactions every day), he set several "records" in terms of achievements, assignments, and promotions. In his early years as Marketing Assistant, I placed Walter in some of our most important projects, such as our big Spanish-language media thrust and selected special sporting event sponsorships in southern Georgia and the Florida Panhandle. In 2008, I promoted Walter again: to become Costco's youngest-ever Assistant Brand Manager. We still interact daily—he's my right-hand man—so I know more about his impact than anyone who's worked with him.

• I have known Karen since her first day at the Patent and Trademark Office (PTO), three years ago, in March 2006. Although I am not Karen's direct supervisor, our relationship is one of Supervisory Patent Examiner to Patent Examiner. Several factors qualify me to accurately appraise her performance and career potential. First, as a Patent Examiner I examined Life Sciences Telecommunication Systems, the same area in which Karen has been assigned since she joined the PTO. Second, I currently supervise a group of examiners in the same technology sector in which Karen's expertise lies. Finally, for the past three years, Karen and I have met twice a week to discuss our sector's cases and to advance her skill base in patent prosecution. Because of my close contact and long history with Karen, I can comment very authoritatively on her skills and career promise.

• I first met Luis in June 2007 through a mutual business acquaintance at Sandia Solar. Luis was looking for energy industry employment opportunities in New Mexico and had very thoroughly researched and begun making appropriate contacts with firms like NRG Energy, Albuquerque Power, and Energetics. I agreed to interview him because of his energy industry experience and outgoing personality, but I had reservations. First, Luis had no experience in our new market: the distributed generation or cogeneration of electrical power. Second, he had only recently relocated from Mexico and his exposure to U.S. business practices was limited. However, Luis so impressed me with his eagerness and research on the problems of the industry that I decided to give him an opportunity. Because of our small size (three permanent staff) and Luis's key role, our frequency of interaction is significant: hourly interaction five days a week. I spent the first three months training Luis for his role, which involved driving frequently together to Albuquerque, where most of our customers are located. Now that Luis is up to speed, he travels on his own, but when we are not at the office together we talk many times a day by phone or while he's at the customer's site. This intensive interaction has been the norm since Luis started, so I am in an excellent position to describe his skills.

• I first met Sarah in the spring of 2006 at Hewlett-Packard in Houston, Texas. She was a new hire (by my manager) to our Pro-Liant DL server technical sales team. I was assigned to her as a professional mentor because I had been leading our team in sales, and my manager wanted "the best to coach the best." As Sarah's mentor for 18 months, I interacted with her all day long, five to six days per week. Our normal schedule for many months was to meet for coffee to plan the day, and then proceed to various sales and technical meetings where Sarah would watch, learn, and participate. Sarah and I stopped working together on a daily basis after she was promoted to team leader for our product group in San Diego last fall. During that period and until Sarah left HP, we spoke three to four times a week on transaction-related matters. We've kept in touch since Sarah joined Lenovo, sharing lunches and laughs. This long relationship has given me a very good foundation for commenting on Sarah's abilities and potential.

• As Logistics Chief for the Army's 20th Support Command, I have known Tim Sparrow since June 2006, when we were assigned to prepare for missions overseas supporting Operation Iraqi Freedom. Tim was the next senior officer in line. He verified that there was a system in place to address all of the command's logistical needs at every transport location from Maryland to the Middle East. Tim was in charge not only of logistical planning but also of life support requirements (food, water, billeting, health and comfort requirements, etc.) at every stage of movement until we arrived at destinations in Iraq. His decisions affected over $20 million in equipment and costs. Tim and I worked side by side together at Aberdeen Proving Ground in Maryland; in three convoy operations in Kuwait; and then in at least three different areas in Iraq (logistics and CBRNE [Chemical, Biological, Radiological, Nuclear, and High Yield Explosives] operations). We not only moved the 20th Command's entire staff but five ancillary units as well. In other words, we moved close to 2,500 personnel, not to mention their motor pools and ours. I stopped working with Tim when he was reassigned to 20th Command HQ in Maryland in April of 2008.

Perfect Phrases for Extracurricular, Community, or Volunteer Recommenders

• As ChildFund's country director in Sierra Leone, I have known Kimberly for two years and directly supervised her from June 2008 to September 2009 on a project she initiated and drove for Child-Fund International in Freetown, Sierra Leone. Mr. Joseph Bright, at ChildFund's headquarters in Virginia, introduced me to Kimberly via e-mail in March 2008. Kimberly presented an ambitious vision—to develop and implement an IT curriculum in one of our model schools, situated in a small village, Koromasilaya, roughly 200 kilometers northeast of Freetown. I had a similar vision but had not been able to find the time or support to fully pursue it. Thus, I was glad Kimberly found me. After months of discussion, we finally agreed to directly bring her on board as a volunteer, bypassing the formal application process. We covered her lodging costs and provided her with a monthly living stipend for the three months until her summer term vacation ended. During her time in Sierra Leone, I interacted with Kimberly every day through e-mail, phone calls, and regular face-to-face meetings. I can speak about her lasting impact on the villagers of Koromasilaya in great detail.

• I came to know Justin McWirth through a classmate at Indiana University, who asked if I might be willing to allow a student to come and observe me in my optometry practice. Our office has an open-door policy, so I am always more than willing to help individuals such as Justin gain exposure and advance their understanding of the profession. Justin was so enthusiastic about learning all he could from my practice that I have invited him to continue coming in and observing whenever he wants. Over the past 14 months, as Justin has shadowed me and my staff over more than 50 hours, I have come to know him both professionally and personally. We have had several lunches together and many personal conversations, and I now consider Justin a friend.

• As Chairman of the Board of Directors for the International Nasal Polyposis Association (INPA), I have spent three years working with Han and can attest to her unique and effective work style. I first met her in 2007, when I developed the rare nasal condition nasal polyposis (NP), and Han—a fellow NP sufferer whom I met through my clinic—offered to help me research our condition and find the best specialists. Han served as a counselor to me, but I also witnessed her compassion and comfortable communication style as I accompanied her on information sessions to educate other sufferers. As it was important for Han to formally extend her knowledge to the community, in 2008 she took the initiative to found INPA and publish the very first website on Nasal Polyposis (inpa.org). In what has been an energizing volunteer commitment for both us, Han and I worked together to develop a business plan, strategize, recruit other board members, and build an organization that now boasts 3,500 members.

Perfect Phrases for Peer Recommenders

• Matt and I developed our relationship during our college years. After graduation, we charted our career paths—Matt went to Wells Fargo, and I decided to start an online admissions consulting business, getin.com. After struggling through the initial start-up phase, I began to look for someone who would be interested in our nontraditional business model yet also bring specific skills in finance. Knowing that Matt was on the investment banking fast track, in 2007 I asked him if he would be on the lookout for someone to fill a V.P. of Finance/New Business Development position with getin.com. I was pleasantly surprised at his response: "Why not me?" In addition to our business relationship, I am happy to have deepened my personal friendship with Matt over the past two years. Aside from our multiple daily interactions at getin.com, I see him socially every couple of weeks or so. I'm proud to know him very well.

• Janet and I essentially started our careers together. In June 2006, she joined the Cypress Hills Veterinary Clinic, a mixed animal practice where I worked as a Research Technician, Kennel Attendant, and Office Manager (it's a small practice). At the time, Janet had just received her license as an Animal Health Technician, and I was a recent graduate of Texas A&M College of Veterinary Medicine. Dr. Amanda Martinez, owner of the clinic, was so impressed by Janet that she hired her right out of Veterinary Technical School, before she had even taken her boards. Janet and I were in charge of the clinic's entire behind-the-scenes operation, while Dr. Martinez saw outpatients. The majority of our days, and often our nights, were spent performing surgeries and caring for critically ill and injured animals. Janet prepared, assisted, and closed most of our surgeries, which ranged from spaying and neutering to tumor and bowel resections, ear hematomas, and laparotomies. She also took radiographs and performed lab tests (blood smears, cell counts, parasite analysis). I have seen the quality of her work and her care every day for the past three years.

• I was Frank's business partner from April 2007 to January 2009. After first meeting through our neighborhood church, we started netwine.com, an online wine distribution business, raising seed money and guiding its growth together. We lived and breathed Internet wine sales 12 hours a day, side by side. About six months after starting NetWine, the company had grown to a point where Frank and I decided to divide the responsibilities so we could increase our effectiveness by focusing more on our own strengths. Frank decided to manage the sales and marketing part of the firm because that's where he earned his degree and had previous work experience. Based on my background in computer science, I managed our website development and programming team (as technical director) and also took care of our accounting and other administrative duties. Because I owned a larger share of the company (in addition to the seed money that we raised, I had invested my own personal and family funds), I was officially NetWine's President and CEO while Frank reported to the board as the Vice President and Chief Technical Officer. He single-handedly led key aspects of our operations, including sales and marketing and the management of our largest database development accounts, which required continuous interaction with clients. I remain CEO today. Aside from our professional relationship, I also consider Frank a close personal friend. I think Frank would agree that the only person who knows him better is his wife, Jean.

Chapter 4

Perfect Phrases
for Ranking Applicants

Your applicant's schools may not require you to attach a number—a percentile rank ("top X percent")—to your esteem, but doing so can communicate in a very credible way that you think the world of your applicant (provided the rank is relatively high, of course). Just as the hard numbers of GPA and test scores help schools separate the accepted applicants from the dinged, so too a numerical rank and a well-defined comparison pool can help schools decide which of two promising applicants deserve the nod. If you are writing a composite or premed/health professions committee letter or if you are a premed advisor writing a letter for a medical school applicant, then you may be required to explicitly rank your applicant. Even if you are not, providing a ranking is a good way to give your letter credibility.

The explicit description of the group against which you're comparing the applicant should be as specific as possible: "the 25 peers in Wue's consultant training cohort," "the more than 20 research assistants I've worked with in my career," "the 150 premed students I've advised." If you are an academic, you can add significant value to your ranking statement by comparing the applicant to previous applicants you have recommended to the applicant's target school: "Sharena is easily the most talented of the 15 applicants I've recommended to your school in my career." Or better still: "Sharena compares quite favorably to Ron Birkenstock, who earned his J.D. from your school last year, as well as to two of my other recent former students, who are now at Penn and UCLA Law."

If the applicant's target school has had good reason to value your evaluations—because your applicants have succeeded there—then these school-specific comparisons can be a very effective part of your letter. If you are an educator at a lesser-known school or university or have never recommended anyone to the applicant's target school, providing information about how the applicants you have recommended have done in school or afterward can help the applicant's target school gauge the quality of your recommendation. Even mentioning students you have recommended who *didn't* get into prestigious schools but later built successful careers can help you establish that you are a recommender whose evaluations deserve attention.

If you are an employer, you can rank your applicant by his peers in the hiring class that started at your organization together, by comparing him to everyone you've worked with in a particular role or position ("all the analysts I've worked with in my career"), or even by referring to his performance in periodic employee performance reviews.

It's probably safe to assume that any percentile rank outside the top 20 to 25 percent is unlikely to impress the admissions committee. So if your applicant doesn't make that cut, you could consider omitting the ranking if the school doesn't require it.

For simplicity's sake, we divide the following perfect phrases for ranking applicants into applicants who have not yet graduated from college and those who have already started their postcollege careers.

Perfect Phrases for Ranking College-Age and Younger Applicants

- In my 25 years as an ice hockey coach at Northeastern High School, I have worked with hundreds of exceptionally talented young men who have gone on to enjoy remarkable success athletically, academically, and professionally. I have personally recommended to your university three individuals who are now playing professionally in the National Hockey League and many more who have gone on to substantial careers as doctors, lawyers, and business leaders. Even when compared with this exceptional cohort, Daniel is one of the finest young men I have ever had the pleasure of coaching. He is at least the equal in character and intelligence of Raymond Nazarene and Ron Lawrence, whom I successfully recommended to your program last year.

- Since my promotion to Courtroom Supervisor, Juvenile Division, of the Milwaukee County Office of the Public Guardian in 1999, I have supervised six staff attorneys, five interviewers, and about three dozen law students (clerks). In my 10 years in this position, I've supervised or worked alongside close to 50 law clerks, so in this letter I am comparing Angela's performance to a large, talented, and relevant pool of peers. She easily ranks in the top 2 percent of that group. I am certain Angela would stand in the top quarter of any rigorous law program.

• The purpose of the U.S. Naval Academy is to provide intensive academic and leadership training for an elite group of future officers who will eventually lead's America's naval defense. It is a demanding program, and we take great pride in the preparation we give each of our future officers. The fact that Joshua not only earned admission to our program but ranked in the top 16 percent (14th out of 86 cadets) of his cohort reflects the very high confidence I place in his abilities and his leadership potential. In his four years at the academy, Joshua excelled in both the general academic curriculum—for example, in digital techniques and control systems—and in such military-oriented courses as naval tactics and leadership. He finished first academically among all students in his Naval Architecture major.

• As a premed advisor for Northern Arizona University (NAU), I typically advise over 75 premed students annually for the premedical committee. Juan Suarez ranks in the top 5 percent academically of my 2008 class of 73 students. His 3.76 GPA in his chemistry major is the third-highest in the department, and he earned the highest grade of any student in his general chemistry class and the fourth-highest grade in his organic chemistry class. In his minor, philosophy, he has maintained a 3.8 GPA, and his paper on the ethics of euthanasia has been nominated for the university's Kopplin Prize for undergraduate writing. Though he is a graduating senior, he has been accepted into the Arizona Maximizing Medical Education Potential summer program because he is the first person in his immediate family to attend college. I would compare him favorably to Jose Aguilar, Kathy Sullivan, and Ryan Pescio, who were admitted into your program from NAU last year.

• Heng took my Introduction to Epistemology course in 2008 and then my seminars on Kant and Heidegger in 2009. Though her comments and performance in my epistemology course certainly established her as one of my more engaged and capable students, it wasn't until the two seminars in 2009 that I gained a clear picture of the quite remarkable maturity and incisiveness of her mind. When she asked me to be her bachelor's thesis advisor, I was happy to comply. During its gestation, Heng sought my counsel frequently, and I came to know her rather well. Having voted to award her thesis, "Habermas and Derrida: Notions of the Absurd," with the University Scholars Prize, I am comfortable stating that Heng is one of only three students I've taught in 25 years whom I believe is destined to leave their mark on philosophical thought in the American academy.

• Don't let Sidney's uneven transcript fool you. As his transcript shows, in summer 2008 he participated in a program at Manitou High School that enabled him to take three courses at Thousand Lakes College, where he earned a 4.0 GPA. The following year, he maintained a 3.42 average (including demanding precalculus and science courses) in the semesters when he was not distracted by his duties as starting quarterback for our Chiefs football team. Moreover, up to Sidney's senior year, his transcripts show an upward trend in performance, especially in science and math classes. Finally, I believe he successfully offset his poor grades in English and history by retaking them last year (earning Bs in both). Finally, please note that he's currently taking an Advanced Placement physics class and doing well. When you view his transcript in the light of his heavy football schedule, Sidney is academically equal to Luke Diebold, whom you admitted two years ago.

Perfect Phrases for Ranking Postcollege Applicants

• My goal in creating the Associate Program Manager position is to groom someone to perform my duties as director so I can move on to other challenges. I thought highly enough of Julie's potential to become a director—one of only three in the entire Strategic Integration department—to hire her, and my esteem for her potential has only grown since. I can confidently rank her among the top 10 percent of all 57 nondirector-level professionals in the department. Fewer than 10 people across General Dynamics's entire staff of 125,000 have the responsibilities that Julie does.

• Out of about 100 officers I've worked with in my 30+-year career, Keith rates in the top 10 percent. Of the 12 logistical officers at his rank or lower that I've worked with, he is in the top 5 percent. Among all Marines, I would definitely rank him in the top 1 percent. In fact, of the 20 officers I've worked with who hold *higher* ranks than Keith, I would place him in the top quarter despite his relative lack of large-unit leadership experience. He is a true servant leader, with one of the best tactical and resource-maximizing minds I've ever encountered.

• As Regional Restaurant Manager since June 2007, I have had the opportunity to work with 17 Assistant Managers at Baja Fresh and am part of the hiring process for all employee positions. As a Training and Development Specialist for Fresh Enterprises since 2003, I have trained more than 63 managers through the 14-week Baja Fresh Management Training program (12 weeks were on-the-job training, which Andrew completed in Irvine, California, and the remaining 2 weeks were completed at the Corporate Training Facility in Cypress, California). Andrew attended this program in June 2008 and exceeded all expectations. He was clearly at the top of his class of nine. During the equipment repair module, he was also able to demonstrate unique approaches to fixing equipment, which he had learned while working with older equipment at our store in Chula Vista. Naturally, Andrew passed the final written examination with a high level of detail and demonstrated proficiency, earning a score of 92 percent, the highest in his class.

• Only about 100 engineers share Carl's seniority level at Oracle. He is a Senior Software Engineer Grade 10, a level that only proven, experienced, and highly accomplished engineers can attain in the corporation. (It is also the same grade as junior managers, who typically manage between six and nine permanent employees.) Engineers above Grade 10 are typically pioneer researchers and scientists who have made lifetime contributions to high technology. Senior Software Engineers receive assignments from management only in the form of certain defined objectives and are then evaluated by their success in attaining these objectives by whatever methods they define. This is an elite group of self-directed engineers, and Carl is clearly among its top 5 percent.

• As one of my very best researchers, Pamela did not have many weaknesses that needed identifying. In our internal rating, she received the "F" notation on her last five evaluations, which means "Far exceeds requirements," our highest category. Only on her first evaluation did she receive an "E" ("Exceeds requirements") rating. As such, among 30 researchers I have evaluated since joining Jewison Oncology Research Center, Pamela is in the top 2 percent in all criteria. Moreover, although by seniority (years worked) she only ranks in the top 50 percent, she is already the fourth-most senior researcher in the Molecular Oncology group and has played a pivotal role in building the team to its current size. She is a superbly talented scientist.

• Since Ryan started his career at United Technologies' (UT) Technical Leadership Program and later moved on to a Services Materials Application Engineer position, his benchmark peer group is graduates of the UT Development Program who have been out of the program for two to five years and serving in engineering, sales and marketing, operations, and finance roles. These graduates have a total of five to eight years of postgraduate experience—in other words, substantially more than Ryan. Another calibration point to consider in this benchmark standard is that UT's Development Program targets the top 10 percent of all new college graduate candidates. (Though Ryan's undergrad GPA was a relatively unspectacular 3.24, he won our attention through his exceptional performance as a co-op.) I am also benchmarking Ryan against my own experience, which includes 16 years of leadership experience at UT across engineering, marketing, sales, finance, and customer service functions, as well as an executive M.B.A. from Pepperdine University. A fellow vice president remarked to me last week, "You're lucky Ryan's on your team; he's one of our best." I agreed.

Chapter 5

Perfect Phrases for Growth and Career Progress

All schools, from colleges to graduate programs to professional schools, seek applicants who are capable of developing their skills and show the exciting signs of accelerating promise. However, they also understand that few of us were born with a full awareness of what it takes to succeed academically or professionally. They will forgive early academic or career weakness if the later trend was upward. In this chapter, we focus on perfect phrases that demonstrate such growth, whether it's steadily improving grades after a shaky freshman year or the evidence of a "fast-track" professional career—early promotions, special management training programs, unusual raises and bonuses. By painting a compelling picture of your applicant's snowballing momentum toward success, you help the schools make the logical deduction: the best is yet to come.

We divide the examples in this chapter into perfect phrases for applicants who are college age or younger and perfect phrases for those who have already started their careers.

Perfect Phrases for College-Age or Younger Applicants

• Eric has shown the ability to continually improve his performance. Eric had a tough time adjusting to the academic demands at Wright High School. I have advised students at six schools in the Wilmington system, and, as a recently designated Achiever Magnet school, Wright is clearly the most academically demanding. Eric struggled with a slightly above average GPA during his first year and started doubting his abilities. Receiving academic counseling from myself and two of my student staffers, he corrected his study habits and limited his involvement in sports. Attending tutorials and help sessions, he averaged Bs during his sophomore year, and during his junior year took four especially challenging courses, including a physics class and an Advanced Placement economics courses. This fall, he's taking two AP classes, and his GPA is the highest of my advisees. Eric has come a long way, and I'm proud of him.

• Although Sandy was relatively quiet in my chemistry class, she excelled in it (A−) and judging from our office visits seemed to enjoy a course that many premed students fear. Moreover, as a former humanities major who decided on premedical studies relatively late, Sandy demonstrated a drive and seriousness in my class's lab that inspired me to offer her the opportunity to work in my laboratory. My lab's TA told me that Sandy interacted well with others and followed experimental protocols correctly. In the following fall semester, Sandy enrolled in my more difficult chemistry lecture and lab. Despite working a 30-hour-per-week job, Sandy received among the three highest grades I awarded that semester (she also earned an A in the lab portion, which I did not teach). I was amazed to learn from Sandy only recently that she suffers from attention deficit disorder. It's an obstacle she has overcome impressively.

• Because of University of Iowa's status as one of the top baseball programs in the country, I try to coach only recruited players, most of whom I've been scouting since they were in the 10th grade. It is rare for anyone to escape our rigorous scouting and recruiting system, so I hesitate to let nonrecruited athletes practice with the team. In January 2009, I was fresh from co-coaching the U.S. Olympic team to a bronze medal in Beijing when one of my coaches told me about a young man, Terry Jenkins, who had inquired about walking on to our team. He had seen him play and felt I should give him a chance. Our team is well crafted and tightly knit, and we do not need extra players for practice, so it was with some skepticism that I allowed Terry into that first practice, our notorious "two-mile track test." The other players knew it was coming and had been preparing all winter; Terry had not. To my surprise, Terry's time was as competitive as his spirit. That was only the first of many surprises. Terry practiced with us for the next four weeks and held his own—batting .326 with power and fielding flawlessly. In February 2009, I therefore named Terry to the team as my utility infielder. Since our primary goal is to win a national championship, each player must make and sustain a positive impact toward that goal. Terry's leadership, competitiveness, work ethic, and, most important, consistency had such a positive impact on our Hawkeye team that I felt comfortable offering him a full scholarship the following year—the first time I've ever done that for a nonrecruited player. This speaks volumes about Terry's drive and potential.

• Though "only" an intern, Teresa inspired our account reps to spend the time and effort to learn and to utilize her services. Our account reps are a competitive bunch and closely guard their client lists. So the fact that five of them let Teresa accompany them on sales calls (something no other intern has been allowed to do) shows how much trust she earned. Because Teresa was so good at back-office and sales data number crunching, our reps had more time to network and grow their lead lists. In the three months of her internship, Teresa worked closely with five reps. When the summer 2009 sales season ended, these same five reps had posted the highest percentage improvement in sales over the previous three months. Lenny Alvarez specifically credited Teresa's logistical support with making it possible for him to win a six-figure account with Dominion Growers. Because of Teresa's services, our whole team was able to give higher quality sales service, increase sales by 6 percent, and improve our repeat-customer close rate by 10 percent. It's no exaggeration: Teresa Lucas is the intern who made Santos Distributors half a million dollars!

• Because of Doug's performance, within a year of being hired we promoted him to Assistant Store Manager, giving him responsibility for the daily functioning of our store's entire inventory and purchasing system. He held this position until leaving the company in December 2008. In this time, Doug completely reorganized and digitized our stock room inventory and labeled the areas for easier weekly counting and daily use. (Wendy's Corporate was constantly changing item codes, which made inventory continuity challenging.) When I saw his finished project and database, I immediately saw its ramifications for our productivity and purchasing cost control. Because of its benefits and ease of use, all the Wendy's in our district now use it today. If Doug stayed at Wendy's, he'd be the youngest store manager in the region.

• I first met Dennis in 2008 when I was coaching varsity football part-time at Mattapan High. He was smaller than most of the players, but he was the team captain. The other coaches laughed when they told me he had started on varsity at nose guard in his sophomore year, weighing a mere 150 pounds. Despite his size, Dennis could get the whole team motivated with his Lombardi-esque pregame speeches, but mostly he inspired his teammates by working the hardest in practice. I still remember the head coach telling the team one day after practice, "If I had 11 Dennis Griffins out here, we'd win every single game, no question." By the end of the season, I wasn't surprised that Dennis was named an All-Conference and All-County football player. He's come a long way from the scrawny sophomore nose guard the coaches used to joke about.

Perfect Phrases for Postcollege Applicants

• When Joyce began working directly for me in January 2006, she was already attaining an unusual level of career advancement for Boeing and for the aerospace industry. At that time she was a sixth-level employee and I was (and still am) a director. Typically at Boeing, there is an eighth-level manager and perhaps a seventh-level supervisor working between a director and a sixth-level employee. I would only have worked directly with a sixth-level employee if I felt she was performing at a higher level than her position implied. Joyce's success in her current role as Composites Work Flow Coordinator is all the more remarkable in that she is functioning essentially in an industrial engineering position, though her training is in business administration. I saw her initiative and managerial potential and allowed her to represent me on conference calls and to work on action plans for me when we did not meet the Commercial Airplanes Group's timelines. I also looked to Joyce to represent me and Production Control & Logistics as a whole during planning meetings. Over time, my confidence in Joyce's ability to handle a variety of tasks grew, and I asked her to work on scheduling issues for me (my area of expertise) as well as on premium freight. Today, as Composites Work Flow Coordinator, Joyce addresses the requests I receive from Boeing plants for me. Her managerial skills have resulted in her steady progress and increasing responsibility: she is now a seventh-level manager, only two levels from director level. Joyce clearly has the potential to obtain an upper-management position and is on track for those heights at Boeing, a statement that can be made about only a handful of her peers.

- As Jason Lee's supervising pastor, I can attest to the impact he has made at First United Presbyterian Church through his dedication, gift for counseling, and communication skills. Jason has ministered to 100 church members in activities ranging from pastoral visits to the homes of ill or needy congregants, leading morning services twice a month, counseling congregants with spiritual and personal issues, and working toward completion of his theological study project. Jason approaches all these responsibilities with a devotion I have rarely encountered in 20 years of pastoral work. When one of our congregants lost his home in an apartment fire, Jason hosted him for two weeks while he found a new place. On his own initiative, he started a community outreach breakfast for teens on Saturdays that has tripled in attendance in only a year. He is enormously popular among our youngest congregants and always has time to shoot buckets with the boys from Boulder Canyon High. Finally, Jason's skills as a preacher are evident in the increasing mastery he shows in his Sunday homilies, which have been among our best-attended services. I know that over the past 16 months, Jason has tested his belief that becoming a public-interest lawyer is the best way to honor his late wife's work for Denver Legal Aid. If his progress at First United is any indication, he will make an outstanding attorney.

- Stephen's impact at Booz Allen Hamilton was immediate, multilayered, and lasting. His initial responsibilities were strictly technical, implementing IT infrastructure solutions for government clients. However, he had clearly mastered these within a matter of months, so I asked him to take more of a leadership role. His outstanding leadership and maturity on engagements with the Federal Transit Administration (FTA) resulted in two promotions during his four-year career, a virtually unheard-of feat. Throughout his last FTA engagement, Stephen supervised up to 20 consultant and client team members—15 of whom did not directly report to him. Many of Stephen's resources were not even allocated to our project, so the fact that we were able to meet tight deliverable dates is a testament to Stephen's leadership abilities.

• Impressed by Lisa's outstanding scientific foundation at UCLA, I invited her to join my staff and me in researching sickle cell disease here at Los Angeles County+USC Medical Center. She performed comprehensive chart reviews for all our study patients, created a multivariate database using ReDA 2® software, and learned how to read Pulmonary Function Tests and echocardiograms. Lisa's database revealed a disturbing pattern. By analyzing every available echo, she noticed that many sickle cell patients had pulmonary hypertension (PHT), though our cardiologist had not been detecting it in the echoes. Moreover, some patients who were at high risk for PHT were not even being given the echo at all. The combination of sickle cell and PHT is often a death sentence, giving patients only two years to live. Lisa shared her discovery with me, and I immediately set plans in motion to base an echocardiogram clinic at the hospital. Because of the quality and extent of Lisa's data (which included pediatric patients), I asked her to present her data at the April 2009 North American Sickle Cell Symposium.

Moreover, I invited her to coauthor a paper with me for the *Journal of Pulmonary Science* on the statistically significant issues behind PHT and sickle cell disease. Her clinical research career is off to an outstanding start.

• All three of the initial projects Adam worked on were implemented flawlessly, so in 2007 he became Johnson & Johnson Poland's youngest ever Assistant Brand Manager. He has continued his rapid climb since then, rising from Assistant Brand Manager to Brand Manager in a remarkable 30 months and from Brand Manager to Marketing Manager in under five years. When senior J&J managers need to get a special project or problem resolved quickly and well, they invariably turn to Adam. When J&J wanted to win away some of Bayer's huge market share in Eastern Europe, for example, they needed someone to set up an aggressive plan to launch J&J's migraine medication Topamax® in local markets where that product was seen as too expensive. Because of Adam's leadership and vision, Topamax's® market-share objective was exceeded by 15 percent. Adam's track record of turning around declining brands and surpassing revenue and market-share goals has been superlative. As a result, today, at a relatively young age, Adam manages the largest brand group in Eastern Europe.

• After earning her bachelor's in education at University of Pennsylvania, Michelle joined University Academy in February 2008 as an instructor. Because of her extraordinary—I want to say unprecedented—ability to engage our students in her first year, she was rated "most popular" teacher by our students (in one class, *all* her students named her their favorite teacher) and "most effective" instructor by our faculty peer review process. Because she was equally strong at building rapport with colleagues (most of whom are at least 10 years older than her) and implementing some needed curriculum updates, in February 2009 I did something I've never done before: I named Michelle to the academy's Regents Faculty Board, where she, in essence, reviews the performance of the eight instructors in our kindergarten through fourth grade (K–4) program. Her innovations have been enormously popular and effective, and I can't wait to see what else this talented young teacher has up her sleeve. However, she and I both know that she will need a graduate education degree to sustain the career momentum she's shown thus far.

Part 3

The Core Strengths

Chapter 6

Perfect Phrases for Leadership

The ability to lead others is a critical skill in a wide variety of professions, most obviously in management, medicine, and law. But even applicants to graduate programs in specialized technical fields, where raw brainpower matters most, can separate themselves from other applicants if you, the recommender, can show they know how to lead others. Similarly, in college admissions, where applicants are not expected to have had many opportunities to lead groups, applicants can distinguish themselves if you show that they have already flexed their leadership muscles. Leadership is a coveted core skill that cuts across all applicant groups and professional paths.

The leadership examples in this chapter are divided into two sections: perfect phrases for college-age applicants or younger and perfect phrases for postcollege applicants who have already entered the workforce.

Perfect Phrases for College-Age and Younger Applicants

- Jim was a very eager student early on, but later he became an attentive teacher in his own right. He trained all our staff members and taught third-year veterinary students and animal health technician students in practical surgical and nursing techniques; current techniques in anesthesiology, radiology, and laboratory procedures; and dental treatment and prophylaxis. On the college level, he tutored three chemistry and biology courses and even taught his own chemistry class in a peer teaching project at Duquesne University. Jim's tremendous enthusiasm and rapport with others has made him an effective teacher as well as a positive role model for many of his students, colleagues, and peers. I have full confidence that he will continue to demonstrate this leadership throughout his career in veterinary medicine.

- Leadership is one of Rick's greatest strengths. Before each game, the bench players would learn our opposing teams' offenses and defenses as our "scout" team. They would then help our starters prepare for the next game by being the opposing team in practice scrimmages. Rick was meticulous when it came to learning the other teams' offenses and defenses; he would watch endless videos to get it right. He would then lead the scout team in practices and make sure everyone knew what they were doing. This leadership was essential to our preparation for each game. We do not name official captains on our team, but Rick always led by example. As a point guard, Rick was the coach or "general" on the court, handling the ball and running the offense. Though often a bench player, Rick was a true leader on my team.

- I have observed John's leadership skills in the way he interacts with the five students he supervises on the Tremont High yearbook committee. John's leadership style is very inclusive. During the weekly homeroom staff meeting, he always listens carefully to his managing editors' ideas, even going so far as to revise the yearbook's theme (which John himself had created) when a managing editor thought it needed tweaking. He's the best writer on the staff, and he spent a lot of extra time proofing other editors' work and coaching them in writing more effectively. I was surprised to learn that John told Mr. Bauman, the yearbook advisor, that his editors had written most of the yearbook's sports section, because I know for a fact that it's almost all John's work. He just wanted them to get some personal praise from Mr. Bauman because he knew his editors needed it. To keep up staff morale, John also scheduled social events and deadline parties, usually doing all the planning himself. As a result, all John's editors respect him and rally behind his leadership. When the printer had to bump up our deadline because of a technical glitch, John had to ask his whole staff to work over a weekend to meet the deadline. Even though it was prom weekend, every single editor showed up.

- If you're looking for proof of Jamila's leadership abilities, look no further than her extracurricular activities. As a student at El-Azhar University, for example, she was the president of student government. She took it upon herself to transform the existing student government association into a federation that better represented the students. Jamila was a founding member of The Mahfouz Society, a popular Cairo readers club for students. I also know that she was the editor of the college newspaper and a newsletter for the dance club. Finally, Jamila made an impressive impact on the literature students of El-Azhar when she headed the Alexandria extension of the Cairo International Book Fair. Under Jamila's leadership, 15 students invited publishers, organized speakers and lectures, and handled logistics for the successful event.

• During Ben's junior year, he became an officer of the Swarthmore Democrats. When Ben undertakes something, he does it all the way. He grew the club's membership by roughly 50 percent in part by working with a fellow member to bring a political workshop to campus. He convinced no less than Representative Ellen Davis and an aide to Senator Midge Alsop to come and speak about political strategy and how students can get involved in campaigns. Ben also wrote a regular public affairs column in the school paper about such issues as health care and the environment. Finally, I know that Ben also reached out to the Swarthmore GOP to convince the Swarthmore Student Association to set up a voter registration fair for people of all political persuasions. Ben consistently winds up in leadership positions because he loves the responsibility and because people know he will execute well.

• Though just a third-year college student at least five years younger than the next youngest sales rep, Ned convinced me that the whole department needed to switch to Salesforce.com rather than use our legacy sales management application. This ruffled a few feathers at first because Ned was just an intern, and not all of my salespeople are technology savvy. A couple weeks into the Salesforce.com training period, we decided we weren't happy with the trainer assigned by Salesforce.com, so Ned volunteered to teach the team himself! For five days, he brought the team together for "lunch & learn" sessions and after-work training. He turned out to be a natural teacher and got most of us up to speed. Some staff resisted him just because he's young. But Ned won them over because he never masks his intentions or passes judgment—there's no façade with him, just a refreshing earnestness. Whenever one of these holdouts claimed they didn't get some functionality, Ned always smiled his "No problem" smile and patiently troubleshot their issues. His ability to lead by example and instill confidence was recognized by my boss at our annual meeting. And Ned was sure right about Salesforce.com!

• Melissa is a natural leader. To raise money for senior prom and homecoming, she came up with the idea of giving free dance lessons on a tarpaulin spread out on the 50-yard line of Kreiks Field. Unfortunately, on the day of the event, it started to rain like a monsoon. While many started to run for cover, Melissa resourcefully switched gears and, soaking wet, rallied us all for a tarp-skidding contest and school-spirit shoutalong that turned out to be a lot of fun. A local news team even showed up (maybe Melissa thought to call them?), and our watery rally made it on the evening news' Szports Follies clip. That news story wound up getting us more publicity than the dance lesson idea, and we beat Melissa's fund-raising goal.

• The 10 work-study students David supervises are clearly motivated by his leadership. His passion for the university's landscaping department is transparent. He deliberately delegates authority to get students to take ownership—and sometimes pays the price. He delegated to one student the task of buying the right shade of paint for freshening up the university logo on the quadrangle's lawn. When the student carelessly picked up the wrong color (though David had told him the exact paint brand and color code), David had to cancel the whole project and send five students home. Rather than bawl the student out in front of everyone, David later took him aside and calmly but firmly explained the gravity of his mistake and the importance of not letting people down. That student got the message and is now one of David's most trusted assistants.

Perfect Phrases for Postcollege Applicants

• Jessica's successful management style was most ably demonstrated in a very difficult project based in Greece. As part of a $4.1 million launch project, IBM Global Services had contracted to deliver a market-focused strategy for a new mobile telecommunications operator. The operator's ambitions exceeded the market's ability to accept its proposed service offering and its own ability to deliver that offering both technically and cost-wise. Over the course of six months, Jessica led a multinational strategy development team of three consultants, two of whom were actually graded higher than her, and three client team members. Under her leadership, the team delivered an outstanding work product that created a new market position for the operator along with a complex financial model and a detailed strategic plan. Jessica successfully overcame the operator's doubts about her new approach by holding monthly workshops with the client's 20-member senior management team and weekly update meetings with the CEO and Marketing Director. Despite more or less trashing the operator's initial plan, Jessica gained complete client buy-in on her team's work from the operator's CEO and board of directors. I've never seen anything like it.

• Bob's most important strength is leadership, and he demonstrates it over and over again in the way he manages projects, leads teams, and works productively with others. Bob's tax partner, Sheila, recognized Bob's talent for leading people and projects early on and began giving him more responsibility than associates his age normally get. In one case in 2008, Sheila gave Bob complete responsibility for setting the time line, monitoring and enforcing the deal flow, and assigning responsibilities to individual parties for a $32-million restructuring of an REIT. This means that Bob was the de facto leader of a team that consisted of a partner and two associates from Thames Tower Real Estate Group; a partner and two associates from our Capital Markets Group; five attorneys from an outside law firm; and the tax director and CFO/VP of our client. That Bob showed such leadership in what Sheila later called "the most complicated deal" she'd ever worked on speaks volumes about what Bob is capable of doing when he's at the front of a large organization.

• Given the nature of business development work and Bio-Pathogenics' size, Shiv has no direct reports; however, I consider his leadership abilities to be quite strong. When the VP of Business Development relocated to the East Coast, Shiv immediately and convincingly filled the void created by his daily absence. He slid with ease into the de facto leadership role in many key business development projects. For example, he began serving as the VP's stand-in with BioPathogenics' partners, and I can personally attest that our partners noticed no fall-off in execution with Shiv as their main contact. Shiv was quickly promoted to Business Development Manager after only a year at BioPathogenics, and he now routinely interacts with senior people at BioPathogenics and the firms we do business with. Second, Shiv's responsibilities today are extraordinarily broad for someone his age, now encompassing both science/technology and marketing/strategy. He is responsible for establishing and maintaining business relationships with the biotech and pharmaceutical companies who are our principal potential partners and customers, for helping to draft and negotiate contracts and agreements with those companies, and for analyzing the market value of BioPathogenics' drugs under development. He also presents company and market research to BioPathogenics' potential partners, interacts with pharmaceutical and biotech company representatives at industry and research conferences, and interacts with clinical physicians and researchers.

• Only 6 percent of Marines are female, versus 14 to 20 percent in the remaining armed forces. Yet Tasheka not only successfully established camp operations in three sites in Afghanistan but was also commander for three convoys in that theater. In all her convoys, Tasheka maintained 100 percent accountability for up to 52 vehicles and 120 personnel over 18 to 26 hours of continual movement. She was in the lead vehicle and dictated convoy pace and direction. With complete lights-out on all vehicles, night-vision-goggle operations were used, so full command responsibility rested on Tasheka's shoulders. To her credit, all her convoys were efficient and well planned—including running reaction drills to possible enemy engagement. None of her convoys suffered any casualties. Tasheka's leadership was simply superb.

• Helen sensitively led 14 internal employees, medical students, and community volunteers in developing a set of training materials for the clinic's community outreach center. In particular, Helen developed a strong bond with the volunteers whom she had to rely on heavily to develop the outreach and health education materials. She was asking these people to really go beyond what they had been told would be asked of them: knocking on doors, contacting other clinics, manning information booths, and the like. Helen knew this, so she took them out for a few dinners as thank-yous and offered them advice about their health and how to take better advantage of the clinic's resources. She also told us what an extraordinary job they were doing (so we were able to recognize them on our website and in our newsletter) and kept in touch with them after the project ended. As a result, when we needed volunteers again for a fund-raising push last fall, our turnout was almost twice as big as expected. Helen has a knack for dealing effectively and empoweringly with people in an understated but genuine manner.

• In three-plus years, Stan has gone from social chair to national liaison for the Washington, D.C., chapter of Young Native American Professionals (YNAP). This past September, he was elected community relations director of YNAP's parent organization, Young Native Americans United, a 24-chapter organization whose current membership exceeds 40,000. As the community relations director, his role is to help young Native Americans get education and competitive jobs and increase public perception of young Native Americans as a productive force in all aspects of American life. As a member of the eight-person executive board of YNAU, he is helping the organization expand nationally, spreading the word about its 501(c)3 charitable foundation, and soliciting corporate sponsorship for its scholarship fund for college-age Native Americans. This is a remarkable record of leadership for a 25-year-old individual.

• Every group Richard has managed at Century Resources has had the lowest turnover in the company. This was also the case when he became manager of the eight-person sales and marketing team. He shared his vision with clarity and force and leveraged his team's healthy sense of competition to make their positions challenging and minimize monotony. He maintained momentum with noncash rewards and fostered a healthy work environment by recognizing employee accomplishments and contributions and sharing credit for success. Richard was always open to feedback on his performance. He remained comfortable keeping an open connection between upper management and his team, to the benefit of both. As a policy, I perform a "skip review" every quarter in which I bypass the manager and speak directly to the employees. In Richard's case, these reviews were always positive as every team member felt he took a special interest in them and truly cared about their contributions and career goals.

• Marcus is respected by our teachers because he is a strong advocate for their work environment and careers. For instance, when Alice Bennett, a social studies teacher, was given the additional responsibility of coaching the girl's field hockey team when our original coach retired, Marcus convinced Richmond Prep's board of trustees to give her a 20 percent raise. Marcus wanted Alice to understand that her extra, unexpected responsibilities were appreciated and represented a career advance for her. Marcus also developed a career plan for Bert Lameul, who will be promoted, on Marcus's recommendation, from Art Instructor to Art Teacher in March 2010. Marcus is a committed mentor and career coach. Tony Garza originally only taught trigonometry and geometry (10 years teaching those subjects), but under Marcus's coaching and encouragement, Tony has become more flexible and ambitious and now teaches calculus.

Chapter 7

Perfect Phrases for Interpersonal and Teamwork Skills

So much of your applicant's time in school will be spent in groups that hints from you that he has less-than-polished interpersonal skills may prove fatal to his chances of admission. The ideal team player is perhaps the applicant with a friendly, even fun-loving demeanor who treats everyone with respect and inspires them to be their best. But there are many other ways to show interpersonal and teamwork skills, from the ability to interact effectively with peers, handle conflict, and reach across cultural and other barriers to the capacity to influence others and inspire trust and confidence. Whether your applicant is applying to college, graduate, or professional school, you should look for every opportunity to provide evidence of teamwork skills.

The teamwork examples in this chapter fall into two broad groups: perfect phrases for raw people skills, that is, the instinctive human touch that enables applicants to build rapport with others, and perfect phrases for empowering teams, that is, the specific types of behavior in formal group situations that help teams work better.

Perfect Phrases for Raw People Skills— the Human Touch

- Juanita brings a distinctive joie de vivre to whatever she does. She never forgets teammates' birthdays, even going so far as to purchase a cake and a card. She has a unique sense of humor, too. I can still remember the time she enticed David, one of our extremely busy assistant team managers, to help her fix a broken equipment locker by offering him a bag of double-stuffed Oreo cookies. From then on, the team was forever putting sweets in David's path so he'd take care of some problem. We as a team got a lot of things taken care of, but poor David sure put on some weight! With her high spirits, Juanita quickly became the heart and soul of the team, the one I could count on to make the appropriate joke in a tension-filled locker room. I've heard from some of her teachers that Juanita is considered "the funniest girl on campus." That's Juanita; she never says quit, and she stays upbeat—always.

- Sanford always treats everyone with great respect. If a maintenance man spends an hour explaining a pressurizer pump to Sanford, Sanford remembers to send him a thank-you email the next day. If a temp worker is staffed with us even for just a week, Sanford takes the trouble to make the person feel comfortable and not like an outsider. He notices intuitively how people feel. For instance, after I was promoted to be his manager after we'd been peers for a year, he quickly sensed that I felt awkward asking him to provide status updates. So he began providing the updates on his own and encouraged the rest of the team to do so regularly, too. I appreciated this greatly.

- The best way to describe Dirk's personality is that he's the kind of guy who can inspire his teammates to try salsa dance lessons after working until nine at night on a difficult engagement in a remote city. That takes infectious enthusiasm, a natural inspirational quality, and the kind of personality people want to be around. Dirk wants work to be fun, not just productive. So he created fantasy football and basketball pools for the office that have really drawn folks together here. On a more serious note, he has also organized members of the M&A team to donate money for sickle cell anemia research. Dirk passes the good guy test with flying colors.

- One of Christine's greatest skills is her ability to listen. She's in the right line of work because as a customer support representative what she does every day is to interact with people of every kind of personality and listen to their problems. Even among the other talented members on her support team, Christine has a remarkable ability to remember the details of her conversations with others, customers and teammates alike. For example, if she hears from another rep that more customers are encountering a new kind of issue, she will note the trend and immediately sound the alert across the department if her own callers show the same trend. She doesn't miss anything. All of her customer and people skills are ultimately about empathy; Christine can put herself in the other person's mind-set. Just as she has an intuitive ability to think like the consumer, she also makes an effort to understand each teammate's perspective, which enables her to relate appropriately to them.

• Frances is the simply the best team player I've ever encountered. Though all the other members of Bethany Hills' computer club are boys, Frances takes it all in stride. No matter how much ribbing she receives or how difficult a program she encounters, she is always the club's "cheerleader," encouraging the boys and keeping up their spirits with her slightly goofy sense of humor. Some of the boys are a bit awkward socially, especially around girls, so her relaxed presence has been really good for them. She's gone out of her way to build a real team environment outside of club meetings by organizing treks to movies or gaming conventions and even once bringing in an apple pie she'd made.

• Griffin has a natural ease and rapport with people that enables him to interact with every level in an organization in the same way: courteously and directly. He is polite and low-profile, even a little bit old-fashioned. That is, he doesn't try to be everyone's friend, but neither does he expect or want to be called "Sir." Subordinates appreciate Griffin's inability to talk "down" to them as well as his habit of explaining things directly and fully, which makes them feel part of the process. This same courteousness and directness is valued by Griffin's peers—associate directors, managers, and project leaders. He is not above joking with colleagues, but he is known to be honest, professional, and unmanipulative. Griffin's wit and humor have allowed him to accomplish much and offend few at Wind Solutions. Whenever a practical joke occurs—as when I found every drawer in my office filled with chip foam!—Griffin is always the number one suspect (though he has never once overstepped the bounds of good taste). Finally, he is extremely generous in sharing his many skill sets—public speaking; wine tasting; even tennis, which he taught my nine-year-old son. Griffin's people-oriented personality has had a positive, motivating effect on everyone here at Wind Solutions.

• Much like a famous athlete who can draw a crowd wherever he plays, Russell has a charismatic personality. No matter what the activity, people want to be around him. I will never forget my first experience of this quality after I transferred from St. Bartholomew's to Holy Angels Academy when Russell was a sophomore. I was walking with him through the school cafeteria when in a span of a few seconds he was mobbed by friends (male), girlfriends, and teammates. I was amazed not so much at his popularity (I've seen that before), but at his unaffectedly modest way of acknowledging everyone individually, as if it was perfectly normal to have a whole school want to be your friend! Russell is an outstanding athlete and a charming guy, but it is his genuine ease with and interest in people that is the "secret of his success."

• Roberta knows how to handle difficult interpersonal situations in a careful, decent way. On one occasion during the recent Whirlpool-Maytag deal, Roberta scheduled an important presentation for us that was to include some slides she had prepared. She told her assistant to bring the slides to the presentation, but he forgetfully misplaced them. Rather than embarrass the assistant in front of us, Roberta took full responsibility for the absence of the slides, saying she was at fault for not looking after the slides herself. After the presentation, the assistant explained to me that he was the one who should have been blamed. Roberta's simple but humane act reflects the kind of integrity and restraint that all good leaders need.

• Gerald has the same compassion and empathy that I make a point of incorporating into my practice. I do my best to make every patient feel completely at ease and to show an interest in them as people. This is the philosophy of health care I practice every day, with every patient. My interactions with Gerald have shown me he possesses this same patient-centeredness. On one occasion, I had a patient who confided to Gerald that her husband had recently died of lung cancer at 41. She was clearly distraught and looking for a way to cope with her loss. Gerald took the time to engage this woman in a low-key, sensitive way that respected her space but helped him learn about her. It came out in their conversation that the woman had been drinking heavily since her husband's passing and was considering suicide. Gerald gave her the name of a nearby counseling network and later informed me of the patient's distress. Working together, Gerald and I have found a way to contact this women's family, and she is getting the care she needs. It was a textbook case of compassionate, respectful intervention that only a few of the aspiring doctors I've met have the humanity to try.

Perfect Phrases for Empowering Teams

• Shirley thinks creatively, but she is also a good team player. This is a rare combination. She works very effectively with both managers and peers, and she is always considerate of others. In September 2008, for example, a university department manager told Shirley that he was unwilling to allow Shirley and her teammates to make an announced software upgrade for fear of losing data. Instead of overriding the manager, as Shirley is authorized to do, she accommodated the manager's concern by creating a completely new database for him. Her attitude is always, "What is best for the university?" She always makes the effort to include her coworkers, whether it's an objective-focused meeting or an informal lunch or a cup of coffee. Shirley is also sensitive to the welfare of others and always inquires about someone's family or interests. At the university, people typically acknowledge a departing member's contribution by signing a card or contributing toward a small gift. Before Shirley transferred to our group, her Bursar's Office colleagues arranged a large farewell party for her at her previous supervisor's home. Even six months after leaving the Bursar's Office, I still see Shirley maintaining her friendships with her former colleagues.

• A few of Denny's classmates are as bright and focused academically as he is, but none are as generous with classmates. In my classes, Denny was always a gentleman when interacting with classmates, whether it was listening courteously as they stated their point of view or using respectful language when disagreeing. When a classmate who always seemed to be the one to question Denny's opinions missed two classes because of a family illness, Denny jokingly finished one of his comments by explaining how he thought his missing classmate would have disagreed with him. He doesn't hold grudges. I've also heard from Coach Mason that Denny shows this same team-orientedness on the baseball diamond: "Denny and maybe one or two others are the heart of this team," he told me. Denny definitely seems to be one of the most well-liked kids at Antietam High. During our fall senior farewell week, seniors vote on the "best student," the "most well-liked classmate," and some less flattering categories. Only three students from the 150-member senior class can be selected for any category. I attended the event and can tell you that Denny was nominated for both "best student" and "most well-liked classmate." Though he did not finally win, it shows how popular and respected he is.

• Margaret has earned very strong quantitative evaluations on her teaming skills in her 360-degree performance appraisal. In fact, Margaret is so widely recognized as a valued team member by her 16 teammates and countless internal customers that during Safeway's downsizing in 2007 there was an overwhelming groundswell of support for keeping her as a core member of the Supply Chain team. In fact, two other Logistics Specialists with more experience were reassigned so Margaret could remain on the team! Twelve months later, when Margaret gave her notice of resignation, she showed her team spirit again by offering to work straight through our new Supply Chain system's go-live weekend. She remained an integral and welcomed part of this team until the system successfully ramped up that Sunday night.

gin contributing. When Nancy joined Google Maps, our team
ployee satisfaction score had fallen to 60 percent from a hig
5 percent three years ago. From the start, Nancy became a ke
icipant in almost all Google Maps activities, from dinners t
pany outings. She took the lead in organizing extracurricula
ties with coworkers, such as weekly basketball games and go
s. A year after Nancy came aboard, our employee satisfactio
ad jumped back to 75 percent. To reduce the impact of he
re last fall, Nancy planned and executed a transition pla
which she completed all current projects and transferre
t information to her coworkers. Nancy's influence on ou
been sorely missed.

- Sometimes when walking across Northwest Capital's analyst department after hours, I see Larry hunkered down in one of the empty offices with a group of young analysts crowded around him. I once asked Larry what he was doing, and he explained that he had invited a group of promising young analysts and junior people to meet once a week to discuss market trends and opportunities. Larry would conclude these informal seminars by having one analyst discuss the one idea that his or her data were showing had the most market momentum. Other times, he would randomly name a different industry sector and have one of these Young Turks state as much as he or she knew about the sector's trends. I was impressed by this display of professional zeal, but even more so by the trouble Larry went to to mentor his younger teammates.

- Lieutenant Evans has a great rapport with others that enables him to get things done. In 2006, when we were stationed in Bagram, Afghanistan, we had to call back to HQ for support because our rations had gotten low. Lieutenant Evans knew that 7th Air Cavalry was supposed to be in the area within four hours, so he got supply palettes built and certified by the Air Force for flight, which usually takes about four to six hours. He knew where all his personnel were that could assist in delivering the rations, and he found the assets to deliver the rations to the Air Cav's base even though it was 20 miles away and he needed to get the proper clearances, which usually take time. Lieutenant Evans's relationship with Army, Air Force, and Marine units was so strong that as soon he told them what he needed, the resources and approvals were in his hands. So only four hours after calling in for supplies, we got a lifetime supply of MREs plus fresh fruit, juices, and things I hadn't seen since my last leave! A lot of soldiers serving in Afghanistan benefited from Lieutenant Evans's smooth teamwork with the other services.

- Regarding Don's team skills, one of his major responsibilities is to organize major international academic conferences at which university scientists, industry experts, and others can present and receive data on research relevant to the Engineering Department's initiatives. Because of their international and scientific focus, these are extraordinarily complex events that cannot be coordinated by one person alone. Don's predecessors were frankly not proficient in organizing these events. As a graduate student, Don must convince people to cooperate through the force of his own persuasion and personality. He has proved to be extremely effective at getting people to commit to help him organize these conferences and recruit the right people to speak at them—even when the people he contacts may not themselves be invited to attend! Don has used his very strong interpersonal skills to organize four of these conferences in the past two-plus years. Indeed, he's become so adept at pulling these affairs together that when I offered to help him with the last one, he replied, "Don't worry, Dr. Scott; it's OK."

- Because GeoTronics is a start-up, Maria's development team was typically called on to work 12- to 14-hour days. As the senior member of the team, Maria did everything she could to help her teammates deal with this tough schedule. She pushed for various perks such as dinner allowances, sodas and snacks, even cots for quick naps, when needed. But Maria's concern was focused on individuals as well as the team. Occasionally, an engineer would

come on board who had excellent technical skills but ¹ interacting. Maria invariably took these people unde⸍ worked to assimilate them into our culture, by, for e⸍ them lunch or inviting them out on social activiti⸍ sion, she willingly cut short her annual leave whe⸍ her teammates were being asked to finish a rus⸍ it simply, when Maria left, morale at GeoTroni⸍

- Aside from his gregarious personalit⸍ memory and easily remembers names and⸍ him quickly make friends and rise to le⸍ clubs (Drama Club, Choir, and Wii Club)⸍ talent for positively influencing fellow⸍ example, within a couple of months⸍ from Knapp High, he had organized⸍ lacked one. He just has a special ⸍ After the 2008 senior class grad⸍ had made at least six close frier⸍ networking" website so Astor ⸍ with 2008 alums. (A website⸍ sophomore—that was a firs⸍ student.

- Nancy was a strong⸍ for new tasks and was⸍ bers acclimated to G⸍ informally almost d⸍ to see if they had⸍ measurably reduc⸍

b⸍
en⸍
of ⸍
par⸍
com⸍
activ⸍
outin⸍
score ⸍
depart⸍
during⸍
importa⸍
team has⸍

Chapter 8

Perfect Phrases for Intellectual Ability

Schools naturally value intellectual ability and need to know whether your applicant can handle their curriculum. Intellectual ability, however, can encompass general analytical and quantitative skills as well as specific technical competence in a particular field. Recommenders writing letters for a high school or college-age applicant will usually illustrate intellectual ability by referring to academic accomplishments. If you are an academic recommender, you want to keep the following questions in mind when commenting on your applicant's intellectual abilities:

- How well or quickly does she absorb and retain information?
- How good is the applicant at "pure" intellectual activities like mathematics or logic?
- How comfortable is she with complex or abstract problems?

Your applicant's intellectual ability will be particularly important if he is applying to graduate programs in disciplines that typically lead to the Ph.D. Recommenders must be prepared to write in detail about the applicant's mastery of his specific subject matter:

- How deeply and broadly does the applicant understand his field?
- How strongly does the applicant grasp the research methods and/or laboratory skills relevant to his discipline?
- To what extent does the applicant show potential to make an original contribution to the field?

Recommenders supporting an applicant who has been in the workforce will usually illustrate intellectual ability by discussing professional accomplishments that show the pragmatic, group-based intellectual skills that nonacademic environments require. Even in the workplace, the core intellectual tools—dissecting problems analytically, learning new tools and domains of knowledge, using one's mind to creatively innovate—are still highly relevant.

The examples in this chapter are grouped into three broad categories: perfect phrases for academic skills in learning environments, perfect phrases for analytical skills in work environments, and perfect phrases for professional expertise in work environments.

Perfect Phrases for Academic Skills

- It was here at Tulane that Becky got her first taste of biomedical research, writing a well-executed thesis on the exciting field of tissue regeneration, under my guidance. In particular, her work attempted to isolate the genes responsible for regenerating auditory hair cells in the chick and to further understand why humans lack this regenerative ability. It was exceptional work for an undergraduate, so I offered her a position in my lab researching the wound-healing capacity of the human anterior cruciate ligament (ACL). By using the in situ hybridization technique, Becky and her colleagues determined that, contrary to conventional wisdom, the ACL does not atrophy after being damaged but can potentially be repaired. This research work resulted in her first publication, in *Annals of Orthopedic Research*. Becky has an exceptional career ahead of her in clinical medicine.

• At Northwestern, Henry double-majored in biochemistry and economic mathematics, both intensively quantitative. Economic mathematics is designed for students who want a rigorous education in economics or are planning to pursue graduate studies in economics or business. It should not be confused with a traditional economics major. It requires advanced math course work, such as multivariable calculus and differential equations, as well as such economics and statistics courses as Mathematical Microeconomics and Econometrics, which have strong calculus components. Fewer than 5 percent of students have received A's in these last classes since I began teaching them in 2002. Henry received A+'s in both classes, an overall 3.8 GPA in his economic mathematics major, and a 3.65 GPA overall (including his biochemistry major). Finally, during the research project required in the economics mathematics major, Henry analyzed data from the Commerce Department and the

International Monetary Fund to identify the role played by multinational corporations in driving international trade. Needless to say, he graduated with departmental and college honors.

• Learning Chinese is difficult not only because it involves learning an entirely new "alphabet," the characters of traditional or simplified Chinese, but because it is a tonal language, in which entirely different meanings can be communicated by subtle changes in intonation. For these reasons, only a small percentage of students here at San Marcos Academy enroll in my classes. The ones who do are often from Chinese-American families. Alice was the exception. Learning Chinese became a passion for her. She was an eager participant in class and spent hours in our language lab. Before her junior and senior years, she spent summers in Taiwan through a connection she formed with a Taiwanese-American classmate. As a result, Alice's proficiency has progressed from basic to fluent conversation and the ability to read Chinese newspapers. Alice's quest for a cultural understanding of the material was impressive. Aside from her summer trips to Taipei, she researched and presented outstanding essays on social issues, economics, agriculture, politics, and gender. One essay in particular, on homelessness in Taipei, was so good I urged Alice to submit it to the local *San Marcos Gazette* (our local paper), as an opinion piece. The energy and pleasure Alice brought to my classroom was a delight for me and proved to be a big asset in enhancing the atmosphere of my classes.

• Kenneth's overall undergraduate GPA does not reflect his ability to handle the academic rigors of Columbia Law School. During his last year at Macalester, his mother's battle with kidney disease took a turn for the worse, and, as the only child, Kenneth had to help care for her. He took weeklong leaves from school about eight times during that period, traveling the 265 miles to and from Red Lake, Minnesota. This emotionally draining experience, which ended when Kenneth's mother died this past April, is the sole reason his academic performance fell below his dean's list performance in his first three years. As proof, I would cite the senior thesis Kenneth wrote for my psychology seminar. He studied incidences of depression among female college students because his preliminary literature research indicated depression might be more prevalent among women. After administering the Beck Depression Inventory test to 630 students at four campuses and sorting and analyzing the data, he found that 34 percent of the sample indicated clinical ranges of depression and that 15 percent had considered suicide (higher than Kenneth had expected). The professionalism and rigor of Kenneth's study, despite his personal distractions, were impressive. I gave him an A.

• From our first meeting, it was clear that Barbara was deeply curious about dentistry. She was never passive about asking me questions to deepen her knowledge. For example, I recall her asking me whether the reason I rocked a wisdom tooth prior to extraction was to loosen the periodontal ligament. She also asked me if the purpose of acid etching is to increase the bond strength between the enamel and porcelain composite. After I had screened a chewing-tobacco user's oral cavity, Barbara asked me what abnormalities in the mucous membrane had suggested precancerous lesions to me. (I explained that it was the appearance of lesions and abnormal patterns of keratinization that concerned me.) Barbara always shows a special interest in learning the pros and cons of cutting-edge procedures and technologies. For example, she was intrigued by the benefits of Cerec ceramic crowns over porcelain-fused-to-metal crowns. She was fascinated to learn how Cerec technology has changed the treatment options available for crown restorations and how the Diagnodent can now be used to uncover previously undetectable decay. Barbara's questions showed me a sharp mind, a healthy curiosity, and a remarkable enthusiasm for dentistry.

• Mr. Baker's academic performance ranked among the top 5 percent of all my marketing students. Before switching majors to marketing, Mr. Baker's academic experience was primarily in the natural sciences. So when he began studying marketing in my classes, he struggled at first with basic marketing terminology and tools. His strong scientific foundation, however, enabled him to quickly outpace other students once he got his bearings. Moreover, his research background proved to be a major benefit to him when it came to writing his thesis for my senior seminar. He chose a topic in the exploding field of loyalty management. He built a very solid database through a thorough literature review (he cited 42 sources though only 20 were required), which enabled him to integrate the latest research developments to support his thesis. Mr. Baker combined recent findings in customer loyalty research with his own assumptions about services marketing to present an innovative concept for exploiting the increasing availability of Internet access on air flights. Mr. Baker grew into a very literate, thorough, and creative student who impressed me with his willingness to challenge conventional marketing thought. I'm certain that Mr. Baker will excel in your doctoral program.

• Despite being a relative novice to advanced molecular techniques, Patricia quickly mastered them. She was quickly able to customize parts of the Espin DNA sequence to her specifications; clone them into a plasmid; and express a novel, usable Espin protein. This was an extremely complicated and difficult process that she managed with very little oversight from me. Patricia was always ready to set aside her own investigations to help me in mine. For instance, she helped me isolate and identify four previously unknown variants of Espin and then characterize their location and overall function within the body. Patricia was extremely generous with her time and energy, and her thoughtfulness and enthusiasm made her a pleasure to work with. All too often, student lab assistants are not much more than skilled labor. Patricia was able to add value by understanding the ideas and purpose behind her work, so much so that she was able to suggest improvements in the design or specification of her experiments that enabled her to achieve her objectives more accurately and efficiently. Through her formal presentations, daily exchanges with me and others, and lab reports, Patricia demonstrated to me that she is a proactive and self-confident researcher.

• Charlie's intelligence and analytical skills were obvious in the way he quickly understood the concepts I presented. He was always ready to answer my questions to the general class. I made it a habit to give opportunities to students who rarely answered by dire ing questions to them specifically. If they could not, I would always turn to Charlie and perhaps two or three other students. He was very reliable for me. But I truly grasped the strength and range of Charlie's intellect during our meetings after class, where he showed how much reading he did around the subject. When numbers were involved, Charlie was outstanding. During our final class project, I gave students who wanted it an opportunity to use college-level algebra and statistics. Charlie was one of only two who jumped at the challenge. Charlie earned A's in all my classes. His cumulative GPA was 3.8, placing him in the top 5 percent of Minnetonka High's graduating class.

Perfect Phrases for Analytical Skills

• During her 15-month assignment, Cheryl completed an intensive financial review of Mexico's independent car dealerships and implemented a reporting and loan-scoring system for continually reviewing their creditworthiness. Cheryl independently determined the objectives of the project, identified its problems, and used technical (financial audit and IT) skills to solve them. The loan-scoring model she was assigned to adapt to Mexico's car dealership network scored each dealership independently of the others, which in Mexico's less statistically oriented environment proved to be inadequate. To adapt this model to Mexican realities, she introduced such useful variables as future cash flows and new cost analysis components into the model. By changing the approach of the loan-scoring model from an analysis of each dealership separately to a broad benchmarking approach, Cheryl enabled us to use comparisons and statistical clusters to more accurately capture the dealerships' financial condition.

• Anthony's analytical skills are very strong. To succeed as a software engineer at Oracle requires surviving a rigorous screening process and then keeping pace with some of the world's most gifted software developers. Anthony worked on three different teams at Oracle because his analytical ability enables him to achieve a short learning curve and demonstrate great technical versatility. Last year, Anthony wrote, in a matter of days, 500 lines of very complex code for calculating 15 to 20 different query scenarios for our Linux-based Oracle Express Edition. He worked out the difficult logic of the underlying problem and developed an efficient module that integrates seamlessly with our product. Now that Anthony is a manager, he keeps his analytical skills sharp by frequently doing the programming work when his staff is overloaded.

• Linda is able to identify investment opportunities well before other analysts catch on. She was quick to identify Alltel and First Data Corp. as major opportunities. Her analysis and instinct told her that both were leveraged buyout (LBO) candidates, so she recommended buying derivative insurance contracts on each entity's debt if that debt was increased to finance an LBO and then buying stock based on an eventual going-private premium. Once Linda's analysis was done, she moved quickly to execute her recommendation. Her Alltel and First Data recommendations received fast-track approval, and both returned over 30 percent (both companies announced LBOs a few months after Linda's prescient recommendations).

• Rajiv's analytical and intellectual skills were amply displayed in only his second week when his expertise in hybrid engine technology was put to the test. Still adjusting to a new environment, Rajiv crafted a report that provided a highly detailed analysis of the next-generation engine system landscape, assessed the potential value of each for Tata Motors, estimated the strategic time frame in which Tata should roll out products, identified the leading players in each market segment, and proposed a detailed strategic positioning approach for Tata. His work was so solid that it has been presented by Tata Motors to all of our groups as the common basis by which Tata and its subsidiaries should make decisions in the future drive train technology market. I also know that when Rajiv consulted with Tata's Jamshedpur Research Centre to validate his work on this report, they praised it and set up a meeting to extract insights from it while including part of Rajiv's analysis in their next report! Rajiv came to Tata Motors in part because he believes in the full promise of next-generation drive train technologies for India's automotive industry. He has the intellectual tools to help Tata drive "paradigm shifting" automotive technologies.

• Diane's analytical skills are formidable. While we were evaluating an investment in EuroGenetics, for example, Diane used a very creative analytical approach to understand how the company's anticholesterol drug, EbaStat, would perform. Since EbaStat was a follow-on to an existing product, Voxidrin, that was coming off patent and hence open to competition from generics, we needed to know whether consumers might switch to generic knockoffs for

Voxidrin rather than EbaStat. Diane created a clever substitution model that simplified our analysis and became a core part of our pitch book for the EuroGenetics investment. Last year, Diane again demonstrated her analytical skills when she and I developed a "bottoms-up," patient-based model for NeoPharmix's antidepressant drugs. Our sales projections were significantly higher than those of independent analysts, because Diane suggested we ascribe value to *future* indications (i.e., uses) of the drugs as suggested by her analysis of clinical trial results. In the end, her assumption was vindicated by the marketplace, and our projections were fulfilled. Diane's outstanding analysis enabled us to justify a $100 million investment in NeoPharmix, which has done very well for us.

• Chen has an impressive ability to drill down to the essential issues in any problem and then place the problem into the larger context of cost savings. This almost intuitive understanding of the significance beneath "the numbers" demonstrates a very sharp mind. While working within the Manufacturing Materials area, for example, he was able to examine inventory reports to identify $2 million in obsolete and inactive materials. Given that the total inventory was $29 million, this was a significant inventory reduction and savings for Comutrex. Chen also performed a material line rebalancing study that projected onetime savings of $350,000, or the equivalent savings of eliminating three jobs (through attrition). Similarly, in 2008, he discovered that the calculation used to determine our premium on freight was inaccurate. This actually wound up costing Comutrex some money in that the correction worked to our disadvantage, but the executive director of Production Control and Logistics commended Chen for doing the right thing by reporting the discrepancy.

Perfect Phrases for Professional Skills

• Martha has demonstrated her expertise most impressively through her masterful execution of our delicate product development strategy. Though GeoThermatics' technology is advanced, we are at an early stage in terms of partnerships with energy industry firms. Because our technology is still evolving, we aren't ready to sign limiting deals with individual companies, but we need to maintain these companies' interest so when we are ready to "auction" our technologies we will have many serious bidders ready to play. Martha has personally screened the 50–60 companies that have stated an interest in our technology. Of these, she has identified 10 that are good candidates for future auctions and 5 that are very good. Martha's predecessors in her position have all had Ph.D.s. However, Martha's natural intellect and three years of venture capital experience have given her a really outstanding foundation in our industry and our products, and she reads voraciously on her own. When it comes to geothermal energy, Martha "gets it."

• Developing the expertise to educate the financial services community in technologies that are quite new requires the best possible analytical and intellectual skills. I detected these skills in Carlos when he first contacted me in 2007, and he has vindicated my confidence many times over. Five of Carlos's 30- to

45-page research reports have become "bestsellers" among analysts because they offer readers more than just a conceptual understanding of a technology niche—they explain it from the inside, with the trench-level knowledge that Carlos has gained by devouring industry newsletters, interacting with engineers on industry newsgroups, traveling overseas to visit companies personally, and speaking directly to the CTOs and project managers who know the technologies best. Carlos has the intellectual rigor and incisiveness to understand antibacterial nanoparticles, nanopowered displays, and other new technologies well enough to tell industry leaders how these brand-new technologies apply to their specific contexts. I have no doubt about Carlos's ability to handle the intellectual and analytical demands of Harvard's program.

• One of Fumiko's major strengths is an intuitive "feel" for the market. She is not only our main contact at Steele Capital but also the portfolio manager in charge of the Asian fund we manage here. In that role, she selects managers and manages the portfolio and is quite talented at doing both. For example, in early 2009 the stock market did well, especially in financial stocks. At that time everyone, including my team and Fumiko's management at Steele, thought financials would keep right on powering forward as they recovered from the overselling in 2008. But Fumiko proposed in August 2009 that we reduce our exposure to financials. This was a major move and took everyone by surprise. Though we responded that we felt we should maintain our exposure in financial equities, Fumiko maintained her contrarian stance. We finally gave in after she flew to Sao Paulo and personally presented her analyses and projections for future bankruptcies and bank bailouts. I must say that Fumiko was right, as anyone who followed the financial sector last year knows.

• Albert quickly became proficient in repairing aural hematoma, closing wounds, closing abdominal incisions, treating cat bite abscesses, and performing foxtail exploration. Because of his considerable knowledge of feline anatomy, he was especially capable as a surgical assistant and became proficient in performing, under my supervision, most surgical procedures (except cutting tissue). Altogether, Albert was a superlative technician who displayed a skill and tenderness toward all of our patients that I have not seen since. Indeed, he demonstrated a level of competence and clinical acumen that exceeds that of many of the veterinarians I have worked with in my career. He kept himself up to date by attending, on his own initiative, continuing education courses at SUNY Binghamton, often read about and researched common feline diseases in his spare time, and gathered and distributed current animal health information to other staff members and clients.

• Tax attorneys are the business world's equivalent of academics: not only must they solve business problems, but they must also demonstrate a strong interest in the conceptual underpinnings of those problems. During the first few years of a young tax associate's career, he or she must hone his or her skills quickly in order to make a high-impact contribution. When working with new associates, I therefore spend a lot of time overseeing their work to ensure that it meets our standards of excellence. Nathan has been one of the quickest studies I've ever encountered. He rapidly demonstrated an amazing ability to identify complex legal issues, conduct intensive research, recognize hidden assumptions, and make sophisticated conclusions. Today, Nathan consistently provides excellent tax advice on complex securities offerings and M&A deals. For example, in BAE Systems Plc's acquisition of Detica Plc for more than $1 billion, Nathan played a key role in designing the complex deal structure. His skill level is outstanding.

Chapter 9

Perfect Phrases for Writing and Communication Skills

An applicant to a Ph.D. program in computer engineering will obviously not need the same facility with language as the would-be Ph.D. in comparative literature. And while merely adequate writing skills are acceptable for an otherwise skilled physician or manager, they can be a liability for an attorney. Whether your applicant is applying to college, business school, or a graduate program in journalism, however, highlighting strong communication skills can help him stand out from the pack. The examples in this chapter are divided into:

- Research and writing skills
- Oral communication skills, and
- English for the nonnative-English-speaking applicant

Perfect Phrases for Research and Writing Skills

• George's analysis of T. S. Eliot's "Four Quartets" was better than most of the papers my graduate-level students give me. Aside from the effort he clearly invested in researching Eliot's religious beliefs and the poem's extensive critical tradition, George has a remarkable feel for the connotative breadth and nuance of the English language, as well as a scientist's taste for hard inductive evidence over abstract assertion. He also writes with uncanny maturity and grace. Though completely comfortable with the expository requirements of scholarly writing, George is a natural stylist who expresses himself with elegance and concision. I was hardly surprised to learn that he's had some poems published in the *Davenport Review*, a prestigious regional journal. As any professor will tell you, it is a rare thing to be able to say that one truly *enjoys* reading a student's papers. With George's papers, I can proudly and honestly say that.

• Louis's written and spoken English are strong enough to do well in college. Here in Carpet Masters' IT department, we have a process in which Louis takes the business user requirements he's gathered and writes them up into a "business plan" format that usually runs 5–10 pages long. In it, Louis outlines the project's estimated duration, the technical specifications, and the business requirements; the program's ability to perform certain functions such as storing, calculating, or adding a file; and so on. Louis has written at least five of these reports, and their level of polish and clarity is strong, better than some of his much older teammates. I can assure you that Louis can present a series of complex ideas as an ordered, well-analyzed, compelling whole. I'm confident he's ready for a four-year college.

• When I selected Katherine to join *The Daily Bruin*'s staff, she had no experience writing news, but we were short on staff and she was an English major, so I gave her a chance. In her first few months, she came to the office every day to research stories, write small news items, and get feedback from me. On her own, Katherine learned the history and craft of journalism by reading anthologies and taking Prof. Wasserman's journalism elective. Within two months of starting, she was handling our campus arts and culture beat with a story a week. In the spring semester, she got her first page-one byline. Katherine has a real nose for news, but she's also turned into quite a stylist, so this year I've given her a weekly column. Some of her pieces are so skillfully crafted that I'm considering reprinting them in an anthology of *Daily Bruin* highlights I'm putting together.

• Mitchell's bachelor's project won both the Gorecki Essay Prize and the Regents College Award—the first time I know of that both have been awarded to the same thesis. Mitchell's achievement was superlative in every respect. First, in terms of sheer length, he submitted a paper that was almost as long as some doctoral dissertations I've received, though he had only two semesters to work on it. Second, his research effort was extraordinary. His bibliography alone ran to nine pages, including multiple texts in Russian and Japanese. Third, the quality of his writing was better than that of any other senior thesis I've seen in my years at the university. Last and most importantly was the quality, originality, and maturity of

Mitchell's scholarship. He fashioned a nuanced and compelling case that the immediate cause of Japan's surrender in August 1945 was not, contrary to conventional wisdom, the atomic bombing of Hiroshima and Nagasaki but Russia's opening of a second front against the Kurile Islands and Hokkaido. For an undergraduate—indeed, for a student at almost any level—it was a tour de force. I am convinced that Mitchell has a brilliant career as a historian ahead of him.

• Though she had no exposure to the gaming industry, in only her second year at Pacific Rim Partners Evelyn wrote a white paper on Southeast Asia's resort and gaming industry that earned her quite a reputation among our investment analysts. She found sources unknown to our industry analyst in Macau, identified Royal Mekong Partners as a company to watch even before its new Hai Phong casino was announced, and crafted a 1-, 5-, and 10-year investment scenario that management has been following to the letter. Generally, second-year analysts at Pacific Rim don't get the chance to present their white papers themselves, but I greenlighted Evelyn's participation in a gaming industry investment conference in which she gave a poised presentation of her findings to industry folks 10 to 20 years her senior. She's now also exercising her literary gifts as a columnist for our internal investment tip sheet, *Capital Ideas*. Evelyn tells me that law schools seek analytically strong applicants who can write, research, and speak well. She is more skilled in these areas than any second-year analyst I've ever worked with.

• Patrick's interest in sustainable development has been obvious to me since he joined the firm. When we launched our environmental services division, he volunteered to put together the marketing package for it, which entailed a significant amount of research into the local environmental service market, relevant city and county codes, and the like. His finished product was as meaty and knowledgeable as it was visually arresting. Patrick has a real gift for taking the often vaguely expressed ideas of our mostly visually oriented engineers and architects and expressing them in cogent, lucid, "actionable" words. Reflecting his growing interest in environmental law, last June Patrick joined our informal Leadership in Energy and Environmental Design (LEED) study group and has taken online courses through the U.S. Green Building Council to build some environmental expertise on top of his marketing education. In August, Patrick volunteered to draft the detailed descriptions of the development projects and design guidelines that we submit to clients and approving agencies. This required that he research comparable projects, zoning requirements, and general plan requirements and understand the entitlement and approval process of the Army Corps of Engineers, county and city governments, and various environmental groups. Patrick did an outstanding job on this, and all of it was on his own initiative! Patrick's writing ability is even better than his oral communication skills. His spelling, grammar, and diction are almost flawless.

Perfect Phrases for Oral Communication Skills

• Gloria's negotiation and argumentation skills are naturally strong. She was a constant presence in our negotiations with NT

Wireless's outsourcing partners over contract provisions, and she would roll up her sleeves and lead the discussion as we hashed out price and service-level performance clauses. She was always fully involved in that. (I know our Legal Department respected Gloria's knowledge and had confidence in her judgment regarding the content of contracts.) Gloria can make a compelling verbal case when she needs to. NT Wireless had used home-based customer service reps before, with mixed results. Because of that experience, many of us believed they should not be part of our outsourcing strategy or team. Gloria was very steadfast and compelling in arguing that home agents should be an integral part of our strategy because of their cost and flexibility benefits. She never wavered, even when the VP of Sales questioned her, and ultimately was so persuasive in making her case that we began using home agents again, reducing our labor costs by almost $2 million.

- Paul is also an exceptional speaker. In August 2007, he emceed United Jewish Charities' annual fund-raising event. Before the entertainment, he made a 20-minute presentation about UJC to the audience of over 1,500 that left us all spellbound. He has natural charisma and stage presence, as almost every other call and e-mail I received the next day noted. During the entertainment, Paul's introductions for performers were articulate and interesting. At the end of the evening, he brought out each performer again with witty and entertaining ad libs that riffed cleverly off their specific performances. In fact, Paul's work that night resulted in a basic emcee script that we've utilized in every annual event since then.

- Because of Renee's strong presentation skills and grasp of our products, she was our first choice when we finally agreed to roll out the training program for our 3,000 U.S. sales staff that she had been championing. Her motivational speeches to our reps are models of inspiration, and I credit the 8 percent increase in sales since the program began to her. Renee also represents Elite Sports at major industry conferences like the Sporting Goods Manufacturers Association. She is a regular speaker at our international sales conferences in Europe and the Asian Pacific, and she is routinely picked to lead discovery meetings and open discussion forums during our customer advisory board meetings. Without question, Renee's communication skills are superb.

- I accompanied Wade to several of his meetings with prospective donors. He has an incredible ability to communicate his passions in terms that resonate with a particular individual. I still remember a meeting Wade and I had with a San Francisco media personality. Primarily because of the way Wade interacted with her (directly, respectfully, earnestly), her attitude toward making a donation shifted from overt resistance to enthusiasm in the space of 20 minutes. She didn't make it easy for him, peppering him with sharp questions, which he batted back with poise and relevant facts. She was so impressed with Wade and his presentation that she made a commitment of $7,500 on the spot!

Perfect Phrases for English Skills

- Alejandro is fluent in Spanish and could have settled in Miami and felt right at home. Instead, he chose Lincoln because he knew living here would force him to learn English. When I first met Alejandro four years ago, his English was frankly poor. Through classroom reading and writing courses, hours spent with *Newsweek* and *The Economist*, and constant real-world practice with native English speakers, Alejandro has significantly improved his English and communications skills. I can certainly attest that today people have no difficulty understanding him, and his written English has become grammatical and idiomatic. I assure you that his TOEFL score of 280 is no fluke.

• I accompany Hua on our visits to all 15 of our U.S. customers, usually meeting about five suppliers per visit. I can assure you that her ability to communicate in English is strong. She takes the lead in introducing us, leading us through the facility tours, and conducting the negotiations. I can't think of a single instance when someone failed to understand her. Moreover, after we have won a customer, Hua handles all the negotiations over next steps, for example, which components we can quote on based on our capacity, which prices we can offer for a given component, and so on. She has complete facility with the English vocabulary for the technical terminology in all the commodity areas we sell, such as machining, stamping, plastic injection, sintering, and die casting. I also know that Hua travels to Dongguan's New York office for localization meetings and would not be sent there if her English was not fluent.

Part 4

Other Strengths and Weaknesses

Chapter 10

Perfect Phrases for Multicultural and International Skills

Multicultural and international skills are closely related to both teamwork and communication skills: they reflect the applicant's ability to function effectively in groups. No matter what your applicant's career goals may be, the ability to interact effectively in multicultural and international settings is a skill that will only grow in importance as the classroom and workplace globalize. If your applicant hails from a distinctive or uncommon cultural group, your job as a recommender will be easier here: schools will already assume that your applicant can add diversity and an international perspective to their entering class. But recommenders for a domestic applicant who has strong international credentials or unusual exposure to cross-cultural teams or environments may also want to highlight these potentially distinguishing factors in their letters.

The examples in this chapter are divided into perfect phrases for academic, extracurricular, or community recommenders and perfect phrases for employers.

Perfect Phrases for Academic, Extracurricular, or Community Recommenders

• Concerned about Samuel's mediocre grades and bad habits, his parents made him a deal: go on a three-week exchange experience in Kuala Lumpur, Malaysia, during his junior year or forget about their help buying a car. It was the first time Samuel had been outside the United States. He was anxious but told me that when he discovered Malaysia was like a "wild real-life video game," he began to enjoy it. He joined in the local school's lessons and events, and three kids in particular befriended Samuel and invited him to explore with them every day after school. He learned their culture and a little bit of their language, and he really enjoyed their foods (especially satay). Those three weeks not only helped Samuel come out of his shell socially, they gave him an insatiable curiosity about the world. He earned an A in my geography class and joined Burnside High's Asia and Europe student clubs. Samuel's grades before Malaysia aren't great, but after it he's earned nothing lower than a B. We all think the Malaysia trip changed Samuel, which is why he wants to go to Thomas More College so badly.

• One of Brazilians' favorite topics in the workplace is football. When Nick noticed that many of his new coworkers seemed to be aficionados of the game, he introduced a small competition on Friday afternoons to "predict" the World Cup results. The friendly contest quickly became a tradition at Brasilia Minerals, and Nick made a lot of new friends there because of it. When Nick's internship ended, his whole department treated him to a match at Pacaembu Stadium. When a new intern arrived to replace Nick in Sao Paulo, the Brazilians asked us to "require" him to continue this Friday football-results event because it helped employees of other departments get to know each other. The football tradition Nick started was quite a testament to his intercultural skills, and it also taught him the only Portuguese he knows: "o país do futebol" ("the country of football").

• In 2008, Russell was assigned to an engagement that suddenly required him to work in Korea for a month. He was hesitant to go at first because he didn't want to interrupt his life, but he did so for the benefit of the client and Nations Trust. When he arrived, he was assigned to work with a Korean summer intern, Chang-sun. It was the first time Russell had had someone reporting to him at work. Naturally, he faced some cultural barriers interacting with an intern who spoke little English, but Russell broke the ice by encouraging more encounters in casual settings, such as offering to watch a soccer match together and even trying a karaoke club together. I can easily see how Russell's easygoing nature made it possible for that relationship to develop. Eventually, they became friends, and Chang-sun later said that Russell was a big reason he decided to accept Nations Trust's job offer after he graduated.

• Heather's most difficult challenge was the language barrier. More than half of the patients at our clinic speak the Cantonese language. Heather's family comes from Hong Kong, so she understood what was said around her very well. However, her ability to speak Cantonese and to interact with patients in Mandarin, the second-most common language at the clinic, was limited at first. In the space of less than three weeks, however, Heather impressed me not only with her ability to rapidly learn common phrases but by her willingness to make verbal mistakes in front of patients if that's what it took to create a more effective interaction with them. By the end of the summer she could hold her own, and we all smiled when one patient carried on a conversation with Heather for 10 minutes before realizing she was American!

• My greatest concern for Ekaterina, as for any WorldAid volunteer from abroad, was her ability to cope with the living conditions in Kyrgyzstan and particularly in Talas. Creature comforts, even medical facilities, are limited. Moreover, she was coming during wintertime, when heating and electricity are erratic. But I was quite pleased with Ekaterina's ability to adapt to her surroundings and immerse herself in the local culture. Within days of her arrival, she had befriended everyone in the office and made many friends outside—spending hours touring the Talas River valley with them after work. Ekaterina also quickly realized that Kyrgyzstan, a mostly Muslim country, practices Russian Orthodox Christianity quite differently than her parents in Moscow. She visited many of the local churches and told me enthusiastically about the differences she had found. Despite the language barrier, Ekaterina quickly developed a rapport with the Talas school board that she was advising. She was always learning new Kyrgyz phrases to better assimilate to her new environment—the first one being "Bir az jayiraak suylonguzchu" ("Could you speak a little slower?")—and her ability to speak Russian and read Cyrillic made her linguistic transition easier, of course. Ekaterina's capacity to personally evolve in order to adapt to a new culture is extraordinary.

• As a Native American, Craig obviously enhances the diversity of any law school. I encouraged my students to improve their counseling skills by becoming community volunteers. Craig was quick to offer, and for the past year and a half he has been volunteering part-time for Arizona Tribal Services (ATS) in Cameron—a nonprofit agency that I serve as educational advisor. Through the one-on-one counseling and teaching services that Craig provided—including conceiving, implementing, and teaching a family mental health class for Cameron's Native American community—he put into practice the depth of humanity and social compassion I had seen in his written work for my classes.

Perfect Phrases for Employers

• Peggy has a unique ability to understand different constituencies. When she joined U.S. Capital, most of its presentation materials were targeted to sophisticated U.S. accounts and were ineffective for emerging Asian companies, who often have no previous exposure to the international capital markets. Peggy's new presentation concept (in English, Tagalog, and Vietnamese) allowed

U.S. Capital to transmit complex strategies in a much faster and more comprehensible way without sacrificing substance. Peggy's presentation concept has been in use since mid-2007 and is now the standard for both U.S. Capital's Asian corporate finance and its capital markets groups.

• When Sean joined the Shanghai MagLev Train project, serious disagreements and tensions had developed between Parsons Brinckerhoff (PB) and China's Ministry of Railways, and there was a real chance the contract would be canceled. The tensions stemmed from PB's belief that we were not supportive enough of their efforts, while many on the Chinese side felt that PB was being needlessly difficult in identifying flaws in the project's design. But Sean correctly surmised that most of the disagreements stemmed from cultural differences between the Americans and Chinese. In his measured, inclusive way, Sean began educating all sides. He made the Chinese officials understand that the aggressive behavior of the PB engineers was not intended to disrespect the Chinese but was simply the way they went about ensuring the project's progress. At the same time, Sean educated the American engineers in China's ways of doing business. I also recall that Sean spoke to his project manager to explain to him that the Ministry of Railways could not be as flexible as PB wanted because of the internal and governmental audit constraints it had to deal with. I was quite pleased when Sean won approval for weekly senior manager meetings in which PB and ministry managers could sit down with translators present and work out differences. These interpersonal problem-solving skills were absolutely essential to putting the project back on track.

• Tamami's people skills enabled her to translate not only the differences in culture between EuroFoods Ltd. and Ăn Ngon Nhé (ĂNN) Foods but in sophistication as well. For example, ĂNN wanted a lump-sum payment of the purchase price. EuroFoods wanted to pay it in installments of 50 percent, 30 percent, and 20 percent to incentivize ĂNN's management to continue managing the company well. This practice was uncommon in Vietnam, so Tamami used all her skill to help the ĂNN shareholders see that the staggered payments reduced EuroFoods' upfront risk and offered the shareholders greater upside potential long-term. She succeeded, and eventually they received 10 percent more than they would have from a lump-sum payment. As in any deal, there is some mistrust between buyer and seller, especially when their cultures are foreign to each other. Tamami's interpersonal, negotiation, and cultural skills were instrumental in reducing the mistrust and increasing the cooperation on both sides.

• I have been responsible for running operations in China, Taiwan, and Korea as an expatriate. Therefore, I realize that it's all too easy to walk into these foreign environments and play the "ugly American" who tells everyone what to do. This is a recipe for failure. Expatriate managers must show their value to the foreign team *before* they can lead by communicating their openness, flexibility, and understanding of local cultures, customs, and employees. Though Mike is fluent in English and Chinese and had spent a few years as a young boy in Tokyo, his command of Japanese was rusty at first, to say the least. He was also taking over in our most critical time of the year, December to March, so he had to begin performing and getting his staff to perform immediately. When Mike arrived in Japan, the office was totally demoralized, its staff gutted. But he listened, he learned, and he used his interpersonal skills to win people's trust. He treated everyone with courteous respect, relied on his English-speaking assistants to guide him in local business customs, and "remoralized" the office by offering 20 percent bonus increases if sales targets were met. It was really extraordinary the way his people rallied around this six-foot-four American with shaky Japanese. Last year, his Sapporo office was the number-one office in Japan, helping our Japan unit generate more revenue than any other country in Asia.

• After the 9/11 attack, Detroit's Muslim community gained attention it did not want or deserve. Jackson's non-Muslim neighbors became suspicious of the entire Muslim community, though until then they had lived peacefully with each other. The 9/11 backlash was severe. Even in our office, I noticed a new wariness and self-segregation dividing our Muslim and non-Muslim workforce. Jackson must have noticed it too because, though he was only a college intern, he suggested we invite our Muslim employees out for a casual team-building dinner. Though some were noncommittal, all six eventually came, and over the course of four hours of food and conversation, everyone grew closer. Jackson and my company have both grown a lot since those difficult days, but I'll always remember Jackson's proactive instinct to reach across and solve cultural problems. It's why I'm sure, after earning his M.B.A., he'll lead diverse organizations well.

Chapter 11

Perfect Phrases for Character, Integrity, and Ethics

Character or integrity is not only important for professional schools—law, business, and medicine—that have an obvious interest in admitting only individuals with the highest ethical standards. Colleges and graduate programs are also increasingly sensitive to the dangers of cheating, plagiarism, and other academic improprieties on campus. Still, while recommenders for M.B.A., J.D., and M.D. applicants will usually be explicitly asked to comment on their applicant's character, recommenders for a college or graduate school applicant may not be. If you do have strong examples illustrating your applicant's character, you may want to make integrity and values key themes in your letter.

As the following examples show, demonstrating integrity can take a multitude of forms, from an undergraduate serving on her college's honor code committee to a young consultant resisting a superior's attempt to alter a report's findings. The best examples will be tough-call dilemmas in which the applicant had to choose between less-than-ideal options that each posed potential downsides.

We divide the examples in this chapter into perfect phrases involving specific ethical choices and acts of wrongdoing and perfect phrases that illustrate personal character generally.

Perfect Phrases for Ethical Choices or Wrongdoing

• Nathan is not Dorchester High's best student, but he may be our most courageous. I know from our summer overseas studies advisor that during Nathan's teaching experience in Liberia last summer, he was discovered to be carrying U.S. dollars while going through security at the Monrovia airport. This is illegal for Liberians, and Nathan could pass as an African, so this raised suspicions. But even after he presented his U.S. passport, they would not let him pass. In a security office, an official demanded that Nathan offer them a "gift" of U.S. dollars (though, again, possessing dollars is against the law for them). To my great admiration, Nathan refused! Standing up to the senior official and two armed security officers, he threatened to call the U.S. embassy. Though the guards kept him isolated from the other passengers throughout the incident, he successfully faced them down and fortunately was allowed on board literally minutes before takeoff. It wasn't a question of the money, since the amount Nathan had in his possession wasn't substantial. He just knew the shakedown was wrong, and he had the guts to not back down.

• Sue is not afraid to stand up for her convictions and defend herself—even when pressured by others to look the other way. Last year, during an executive board meeting, she was approached by the chairman (a prominent former Credit Suisse executive) during a break. He asked Sue to explain a discrepancy he had discovered on one of the financial charts pertaining to account-balance growth dynamics. Sue was able to look at the exhibit (which she had not seen before) and give an accurate answer, but that answer differed from the explanation the chairman had been given before and was a little unflattering to our senior management. The chairman was appreciative of Sue's explanation and honesty. But a senior executive of Southwest Trust (no longer with the company) later confronted Sue with his displeasure over the way she had answered the chairman, and he asked Sue to go back with an explanation that would make Southwest Trust look good but was inaccurate. Sue refused. I was impressed by her strength in this stressful situation. She survived it, and people respect her for her integrity.

• People admire Hào for his values. He was assigned to handle our clinical trial's budget and grant funds administrative process partly because his professors told us he has an ethical character (he once turned in three classmates for cheating on a biochemistry exam). Throughout the Xinjiang clinical trial, Hào had to deal with local pharmaceutical companies' attempts to alter our findings through "gifts" and other bribes. I can attest that Hào not only personally refused such offers but put in place new accounting processes that make it easier to track any unusual activity or deposit. He is our moral compass.

123

• In 2008, I named Katherine to manage all the performance and scalability tasks for an application that a team of her fellow consultants had spent the past month developing on the client's site. Within days of arriving, she discovered that our application's performance was not consistent with its design specifications. Our on-site development manager asked Katherine to change her evaluation report to me to give the impression of acceptable performance, even though the manager knew full well that the application was unstable. The manager told Katherine that "eventually" his team would ensure that the application did conform to requirements, and in the short term Katherine's report could buy us some valuable time. Katherine refused to "stuff the ballot box" and reported the performance issues to me. But she went further: with my OK, she executed tests that documented the exact nature of the performance problem and took the problem and her solution ideas directly to the client. The project was delayed, and our on-site development manager was not pleased. However, though initially disappointed, the client respected our forthrightness and three months later received a much better product. We're working on our second follow-on project with them now.

• In an unhappy chapter of our organization's recent history, Nick demonstrated tremendous ethical maturity. He discovered that our CFO was engaging in illegal activities to benefit himself financially. Though the CFO was his ultimate manager, with great professionalism and discretion Nick used appropriate channels and documentation to report his findings to me and later to Media-Digit's board, which ultimately asked the CFO to resign. As our executive management team worked to stabilize the organization by finding an appropriate replacement, Nick proactively drew up a report on the process flaws that had enabled the CFO to succeed in his activities without detection. He approached me to propose and institute these changes, which proved enormously effective. We have since presented Nick's process as a best-practices case study for the Institute of Business Ethics. Nick demonstrated to me an extraordinary sense of ethical propriety and political skill. More than anything, his behavior convinced me that his professional horizon is unlimited.

Perfect Phrases for Showing Character

- I have no doubt that Alice has the integrity to be a lawyer. You'd be surprised how many of my students ask for "wiggle room," such as extra time for an assignment or special consideration for a disappointing grade. But Alice never did; she never asked for any preferential treatment of any kind. She always understood what I expected and respected my guidelines, both in her class papers for me and in her thesis. In fact, I actually awarded her extra points for turning two assignments in on time because almost no one else in the class did. Almost every student in the class complained of problems finding a sufficient number of references for a paper I assigned on the Dred Scott decision. Alice was among a small handful who didn't complain or ask me to settle for a smaller bibliography than I requested. In fact, the bibliography she submitted had more references than I asked for and was very, very close to the model bibliography I had drawn up for the assignment. It's a small example but a telling one. Alice's unwillingness to ask for special favors speaks volumes about her character and fitness for the law.

• I have had too many direct reports who just try to figure out what I want to hear and then offer that as their considered input. Bruce has never given me this problem, basically because his integrity won't allow him to recommend something he doesn't believe in. For example, during our geothermal pilot program for the Department of Energy (DOE), our partner, Axxent Energy, approached Bruce to sign off on some reports that we needed to submit to DOE for auditing purposes. Since Axxent was working for us and we had already vetted the reports, their request seemed reasonable, but Bruce repeatedly refused to "rubber-stamp" documents that he had not read. When he was reminded that Axxent was paying us to participate in this program, Bruce responded: "Look, we are international contractors, not local ones. Our global reputation as professionals is at stake, and we simply can't jeopardize it just to make one partner happy." In the end, his argument prevailed, and Axxent has done things by the book ever since.

• For confirmation of Manish's integrity, one need look no further than his decision to leave a well-paid, high-potential job at the Ministry of Infrastructure for ethical reasons. One of Manish's most intense passions is his desire to promote honesty and integrity in government. At university, he was the president and founder of Imaandari, a group of young professionals who motivate India's youth to assume leadership positions through discussions on controversial political issues. Manish also mentioned to me that he is a volunteer consultant for the Orissa Anti-Corruption Front, which is an independent organization, recognized by law, that is charged with investigating cases of fraud and corruption in Orissa's state government. By staying active in his temple and in the larger religious community, Manish also maintains strong family values. Integrity defines every part of his life.

• Bantam Consulting offers employees rigorous ethics training through courses on our code of ethics, managing conflicts, international business practices, and the like, all of which are offered by our Ethical Business Practices Center. Annette took all the required courses in under a year and a half and as a result has become a huge asset for me in handling the sensitive issues that arise in our competitive intelligence practice. For example, last year I assigned Annette to track all the consultancies that compete with us in our niche, though this was her first foray into competitive intelligence. Showing mature awareness of the antitrust laws and intellectual property issues that dominate this practice, Annette set ground rules for what constitutes appropriate and inappropriate data gathering, established rigorous standards for collecting information via third-party firms, ensured that her two team members took all the appropriate courses in our center, and personally mentored them by giving them specific examples of what would constitute crossing the ethical line. For this reason, Annette's reports are models of ethically sensitive analysis that have earned the complete trust of executive management.

• I have total trust in the integrity of Mary's research and legal analysis. If after exhaustive research Mary discovers that tort law is unclear on an issue, she always objectively analyzes for me the strength of each authority on that issue, rather than just drawing the conclusion that's most favorable to our client. Likewise, she interacts with others fairly and scrupulously gives credit where it's due. Mary and I were once working together on a project that required a summer intern to conduct intensive research to justify a change to a pleading. When Mary later showed our revised pleading to the partner, he complimented her on the passage though the intern had written it. Mary reflexively informed the partner that she was not the one responsible for it. Telling me about the incident later, the partner told me how much he respected Mary for only wanting credit she had earned. I too was impressed, but it only reflected the kind of integrity I have observed in Mary since the day she joined this office.

• Captain Alice Stivlin, Peter's former commander in the Office of Naval Research (ONR), thought so much of his ethics that she selected him to lead a complete audit of our unit, from identifying all problem areas in six departments to making specific recommendations for resolving them. Peter spent 40 days inspecting every department, including operations, training, and the ONR laboratory, and uncovered more than 200 procedural deficiencies. Although Peter had close relationships with each of the department heads, and some tried to capitalize on them to manage Peter's findings, he conducted his inspections in a professional, honest, and unbiased manner and then communicated objective and insightful findings to the Directorate. Peter then spent the next 30 days working intensively with each department head to resolve these deficiencies and ensure compliance throughout the unit. After the Navy's year-end inspection, it awarded our unit with the Excellence Award for achieving the highest ratings possible. Peter's ethics are irreproachable.

Chapter 12

Perfect Phrases for Volunteering and Social Impact

Corporate social responsibility campaigns, pro bono legal services, environmental sustainability projects, and free medical clinics for the homeless are only some of the ways in which college and professional school graduates show their concern for larger social issues. Indeed, more and more applicants to colleges, graduate school, and professional school are stating idealistic "social impact" goals in their applications. Usually this is because of sincere conviction, but often it is also because they believe such social concern plays well with admissions committees. One of the ways that schools determine whether these altruistic declarations are for real is to pay close attention to what recommenders say—and don't say—about an applicant's volunteer or community involvement. If your applicant has displayed an unusually strong or sustained commitment to benefiting society and helping people, consider devoting some space to it in your letter, especially if that activity is closely related to her postdegree goals. Such volunteerism shows not only selflessness but often leadership, energy, good character, and social skills as well.

Since social impact activities can be pursued at work, in the community, and at school, we have divided this chapter into perfect phrases for employers, perfect phrases for community recommenders, and perfect phrases for academic recommenders.

Perfect Phrases for Employers

- In addition to bringing a new analytical rigor to his IBM team, Rudy took an active role in corporate community initiatives. In fact, immediately after completing his orientation period, Rudy joined a Community Involvement Team (CIT) to volunteer on environmental projects. Because of his level of commitment (at least 10 hours a week), within six months he was elected to the CIT steering committee, which was responsible for determining companywide events as well as distributing some community grant monies. Within a year of joining IBM, Rudy had been appointed project manager for the fifth annual IBM Louisville Volunteer Day, a substantial time commitment.

- Margie demonstrated her dedication to Providence Equity Partners by volunteering her time not only in project activities but in several local office and community events. Though these projects would occasionally demand as many as 30 hours a week, Margie demonstrated tireless enthusiasm for our extracurricular events, adjusting her schedule and finishing tasks after work and on weekends so she could contribute to events like the Cystic Fibrosis 5K and our School-to-Work-Day program. Margie also took the initiative to co-organize a meeting of 35 "under 40" associates to plan our "Provide Providence" charity fund-raiser project. Leading the planning with three co-organizers entailed selecting and reserving a space at a local community center, soliciting volunteers and keynote speakers for the event, consolidating the overall presentation, and multiple other activities. Finally, Margie has also participated in Providence's graduate school preparation programs and cocreated a graduate school mentor program in our New York office. Her bottomless energy and dedication are a source of wonder to us all.

• Dirk is a friendly, ambitious person with a deep commitment to helping others. His personal involvement in recruiting volunteer business leaders to stabilize the finances and expand the effectiveness of IKEA Community Partners is characteristic of these qualities. He is also the only person at IKEA who has established a scholarship program to help deserving IKEA student-employees pay their educational expenses. Two years ago, Dirk also helped a programmer named Khanh Nguyen improve his career chances at IKEA by strengthening his English skills. Khanh's English was below the average expected for someone at his level in the company, so Dirk personally motivated Khanh to take additional English classes in the morning and afternoon. After eight months, Khanh's English met IKEA's standards, and he has since progressed from programmer to team programming lead in our IT division.

• Vicky's most constructive effort to improve Jacoby & Sonnenstein centered on retaining women associates, a major problem for many law firms today. Though women represent half of our starting classes each year, that percentage usually drops after three or four years with the firm because balancing career and family proves too difficult. At Jacoby & Sonnenstein, for example, only 6 of 21 partners are women. Vicky and I discussed this issue both generally and in the context of her own career. She told me that when it comes to making the fundamental life decision of having a family, financial considerations alone aren't enough to induce some female attorneys to accept the sacrifices required to become partner. Vicky therefore suggested that Jacoby & Sonnenstein establish a direct mentoring program between its women partners and women associates. My fellow partners quickly approved Vicky's idea when I presented it, and for the past two years women partners and associates have held biannual meetings to discuss work-life balance issues. Moreover, today each of our female partners serves as a mentor for a small group of women associates who can come directly to the partner to discuss their concerns. This new program has been hugely popular with our female associates. However, the ramifications of Vicky's initiative have been even greater than she intended. Because Jacoby & Sonnenstein is a large firm, young attorneys tend to feel ignored by upper management until they lose their sense of ownership and just bide their time until they've gained enough experience to be hired by smaller firms. Vicky's mentorship idea seemed a natural way to make work more meaningful for young attorneys. This past July, Jacoby & Sonnenstein launched an informal mentor program in which each partner is matched to one first-year attorney to provide guidance and a sense of "belonging." Vicky deserves the credit.

Perfect Phrases for Community Recommenders

• I came to know Rosa through her personal commitment to support her cultural community here in Minnesota. She established the Hispanic Community in Duluth Counseling Center (HCDCC) with the help of Father Jensen, whom she knew at Our Mother of Consolation Catholic Church, where most local Hispanics worship. Some parishioners needed legal advice and asked Rosa to help them find a lawyer. With her initiative and cheerful resourcefulness, she researched and networked until she found a law firm with Spanish-speaking attorneys, whom she convinced to focus some pro bono time on HCDCC. From this, Rosa has continued to contribute more and more of her time and expertise. Today she helps new neighbors and immigrants open bank accounts, find apartments, secure jobs, and choose schools for their children. For me, it speaks volumes about Rosa that her ultimate career goal is to earn a master's in ESL education so she can help Duluth's growing Hispanic community succeed and grow.

• Philip played an absolutely critical role in making our African Dance Night—our largest annual dance event—a success in August 2008. He believed, rightly, that an African modern dance troupe would be of interest to Georgia State students, and he took responsibility for locating and selecting the dance group Umoja, which uniquely fuses Kenyan and Tanzanian traditional dance with modern ballet. Philip arranged for the dancers to fly over from Nairobi and secured the auditorium of a nearby community college at no cost when Rialto Center was unavailable. He also created a great marketing plan to pack the hall by using advertising and PR and by tapping into our volunteers' social circles. The goal was 1,000 attendees, but more than 2,500 showed up. Philip also worked with other chapters to coordinate Umoja's nine-city national tour and helped create the national marketing campaign. Umoja's Georgia State performance alone raised over $5,000 in Atlanta and over $20,000 nationwide.

• Duan has also shown admirable concern for the community that is her homeland, Thailand. For example, she was passionate about expanding BearingPoint's operations in Thailand and made sure that she was aware of all requests for proposals (RFPs) in Thailand. She personally joined Thai professional associations and registered BearingPoint to get the RFPs of all major companies in Thailand. She engaged in discussions with potential business partners that could represent BearingPoint in Bangkok, and she helped write a BearingPoint proposal for Thailand when she was a business analyst, though this is more of a manager's task. Not least, in less than two years' time, Duan also represented BearingPoint in five job fairs sponsored by the Thai Embassy, which led directly to BearingPoint hiring four students for internships, two of whom were then hired full-time. Duan's passion for helping her country is remarkable.

- This past year, John joined Boston Big Brothers Big Sisters (BBBBS) and "adopted" a little brother. Kenny Soames is a nine-year-old who lost his father to cancer when he was seven. When Kenny's profile came up, John was especially interested in being his big brother because he too had had to grow up without a father. John later told me that he felt he had the empathy to help this little kid who was having a hard time dealing with a huge event in his life. Kenny lives with his younger brother (five years old) and his mother, who works as a maid in South End. Kenny has been having a hard time dealing with his father's death emotionally and is relying on the help of a psychiatrist and medication. When John first met him, Kenny's mother shared that he was having a difficult time in his sessions and at school. She enrolled him in BBBBS hoping to match him up with a big brother, as she felt that Kenny not only needed time away from his mother and brother but also needed some male interaction. John usually spends four days a month (about three hours each session) with Kenny, and in only three months his impact has been tremendous. Kenny's grades have improved, and he smiles a lot more than before. John has a natural rapport with kids and is talking about ramping up his involvement in Big Brothers Big Sisters.

- Claudia's commitment to her community has been exemplary. Despite a demanding academic schedule, she took the time to participate in such community activities as Pet Health Week on cable TV's "Kids Club" show, tutoring early-morning classes and launching the Canine Rescue Club at Carroll Junior College, and participating in the Carroll County rabies vaccination clinic. After a couple of days of observing veterinarians with their patients in the clinic, Claudia became an active participant. In addition to learning about the day-to-day activities of veterinarians, she provided help in patient grooming and hygiene and learned how to use some of our medical diagnostic equipment. Because we are the only clinic in the area, the work environment is hectic, chaotic, and sometimes very upsetting. Through it all, Claudia was extremely friendly and cordial to staff and patients' families; basically, she never met a dog she couldn't help in some way.

Perfect Phrases for Academic Recommenders

- In addition to his academic successes, Don helped organize the university's seventh and eighth international book fair while participating in three student service clubs (Campus Ambassadors, which showed prospective students around the campus; Michigan Cares, which raised funds for state charities; and the International Students Society, which helped foreign students with campus life). Don was also a member of the lacrosse team, which required him to train two hours every day, Monday through Friday, and four hours on Saturday. Because I was the dean of student affairs during Don's final year, I was well aware of all his activities, as well as the energy and dedication he brought to them. Few students are capable of juggling so many activities and still succeeding academically.

- Just as impressive as Tammy's academic accomplishments was her tireless dedication to Peyton High School's extracurricular life. While maintaining straight A's, Tammy actively participated in Peyton Boosters Club, where she took leadership roles in fundraising events, monthly pep rallies, community public relations events, and membership drives. I especially appreciated her big involvement in the Peyton Food Festival, which not only helped the school raise funds but also brought together teachers, coaches, parents, and students from all over Butler County. Because of Tammy's outstanding academic performance and her devotion to Peyton's student life, the school awarded her its prestigious Best in Class Achievement Award last year. I was one of the committee members who voted for Tammy, and I can assure you the vote and the enthusiasm for her were unanimous.

• Pamela's participation in the international bioinformatics community has set an outstanding example for her classmates. She is the Mid-Atlantic Regional Coordinator of the students' division for the International Society for Computational Biology (ISCB) and regularly organizes meetings and conferences featuring international speakers on topics ranging from protein-protein docking to comparative genomics. Her chapter also reaches out to other molecular biology and information technology undergraduates in area schools like Columbia, New York University, and Fordham through fairs and other events. Moreover, Pamela has begun presenting her own precocious bioinformatics research to the ISCB community. She has already made well-received presentations at three conferences, chaired a students' session on sequence analysis, and been listed as coauthor on four papers for international bioinformatics journals like *Applied Bioinformatics* and *Nature Bio-*

technology. Because of her unusually mature and energetic involvement in the field, ISCB nominated Pamela in 2009 to its top 10 list of "undergraduate bioinformatics leaders."

• David's impact on the Ripon College community was multidimensional. As a versatile columnist and reporter for Ripon's *College Days* newspaper, he wrote pieces on local business and economic trends, reported on the university's soccer and ice hockey clubs, and even wrote the occasional concert review. David was thrilled at the thought that his words and opinions were being read by hundreds of peers, but it was his intellectual curiosity that really drove him. He also genuinely identified with Ripon and its community. In his residential hall, David was selected by the resident manager to be a tutor both because of his academic abilities and his willingness to help others. He arranged mechanical engineering tutorials in both his junior and senior year, and in his senior year he was elected dorm representative by his peers. Finally, David has been an outstanding student ambassador for Ripon by leading over three dozen campus tours for prospective students. He is the personification of the engaged student.

Chapter 13

Perfect Phrases for Initiative and Creativity

What separates the exceptional student, employee, or young professional from her average peers? Often, it's basic personal characteristics like drive and innovation. Initiative is simply the willingness to take action when others hang back. Innovation is the ability to find new solutions when others cling to the conventional. These core qualities—the distinguishing traits of success and leadership—are the raw human materials that schools sift through application after application to identify. They will be just as visible in high school applicants applying to college as in fast-track young managers applying to business school.

The examples in this chapter are divided into perfect phrases for initiative and perfect phrases for creativity.

Perfect Phrases for Initiative

• Marilyn steps into leadership roles easily, always to the benefit of whatever project or group activity is under way. She "pushed the envelope" on every project I gave her. For example, when we were preparing for a third round of financing, I asked Marilyn to prospect a target list of venture capital firms. She not only established introductions and set up meetings with most of the target firms, but also moved the process forward by creating and then walking them through preliminary information such as our company history, market information, and financials. Marilyn set up six meetings with leading Silicon Valley VC firms for me, including Menlo Ventures, Telos, and Venrock. Our financing round went off without a hitch, and Marilyn's proactive groundwork was a big reason why.

• One of Anand's objectives was to do foundational research for me on the state of the art in nanomaterials, molecular electronics, and nanoelectromechanical systems. This involved identifying and interviewing the relevant subject-matter experts in the Los Angeles area; exploring their specific areas of research interest with them; contextualizing and collating his findings into a coherent report; and then presenting that report in a compelling way to me and my graduate student assistants. I gave Anand complete freedom to choose the format, modalities, and conclusions of his report. He handled everything seamlessly, with little dependence on me, and delivered an incisive, comprehensive, and mature report right on deadline. Thanks to Anand's self-driving independence, I have a report that has become the key guiding document of my own research.

• What I like most about Rebecca is her drive to achieve and her initiative. In 2008, she became convinced that the key to the success of our supercomputing project was sponsoring academic research in the United States and using the outcomes from that research to enhance our project's legitimacy as an R&D project. She therefore began building business cases for Pacific Silicon's sponsorship of research at U.S. universities. She thoroughly assessed 12 leading universities where supercomputing research was more advanced, worked with me in developing a request for proposal (RFP) that she sent to three universities, evaluated the RFPs we received, and then selected the Supercomputing Center at Oklahoma University (OU) as the best candidate. One of the reasons Rebecca selected OU was that they had formalized a supercomputing applications hand-book. Within Pacific Silicon, Rebecca then began selling the idea of a supercomputing applications partnership between us and OU. She never hesitated to ask senior people at Pacific Silicon for their support and to associate them with the decision so they would feel part of the innovation from its earliest stages. For example, she organized visits to Oklahoma by key decision makers, including the head of our scientific division, the head of marketing for our corpo-rate applications division, and our vice president of R&D. The fact that such high-level individuals were willing to personally accept Rebecca's invitation shows how very effective she was at creating enthusiasm for her idea.

• The only way to get noticed and to progress within a small software company started by brilliant individuals is to market your-self and go after opportunities, not wait for others to hand them to you. Jason was quickly promoted into key development roles because he showed just this ability. For example, he worked with Ostinato Software's former marketing director to develop a sample website for a sales presentation for our software product Orbiter. This meant he had to learn HTML and Java in a month so he could enhance the features on the Internet site. To accomplish this, Jason wrote the applications and designed web pages at home, never letting it interfere with his daily responsibilities. Similarly, when customers complained that creating Orbiter applications was too complex, Jason took on the task of building a programmer's library to simplify this process. The library is now included in the product, which, as the leading product in its field, has earned Ostinato over $30 million.

• My management philosophy is to give my people the freedom to find their own way, with an occasional helpful nudge from me when they need it. In other words, the professionals I hire must have initiative. When I assigned Melissa the sovereign wealth funds (SWF) project, I was basically giving her two months to master and write an exhaustive report on a field she knew nothing about. Melissa responded to this daunting challenge with her usual aggressiveness. Rather than read a few articles, go to the usual public databases, and speak to corporate PR people, Melissa used the Internet to identify the key insiders at Goldman Sachs, Barclays Capital, and others and gathered her information from the source. Melissa's SWF research is now one of the standard reference reports in the industry. Melissa then took it upon herself to send our sales department all the leads she had developed during her research.

She even followed up with sales weeks later to find out if they had contacted them. Finally, after we published her report, Melissa was incredibly proactive in promoting her work among journalists and has proved to be a key asset in increasing the visibility and credibility of our firm.

• One example should capture the whirlwind intensity that Howard brings to his work. In 2009, our Capital Appreciation Bond module had fallen months behind schedule because of the time it took to verify multiple iterations of our test results. Each iteration consisted of two spreadsheets of about 1,000 rows and 30 columns, which our team's business analysts had manually compared cell by cell. A single iteration would take almost a week for two business analysts to review. Moreover, only analysts with intimate knowledge of municipal securities could do the verification. Thus, our entire development team had to sit idle until the verification process indicated whether any coding changes were required. Seeing our deadline slipping away, I agreed when Howard volunteered to take a look. Within a couple of hours, he had recommended an improvement! I told him it seemed risky and time-consuming, but he persisted, challenging my recommendation to postpone his experiment. I finally gave him one day. By lunch the next day, Howard had a rough working version of a program for automating the verification process that he promised would bring us back on schedule. Howard had developed a Visual Basic program that would cycle through the results of the Capital Appreciation Bond testing iterations and compare the actual results to the expected results. Any discrepancies were incorporated into a spreadsheet, created by the program, which would show the expected result alongside the actual result. Moreover, the errors were color-coded to help the business analyst determine the pattern of errors occurring in the iteration, which enabled the development team to begin working on the fix almost immediately. Within a day or two, we had completed one iteration of testing using only one business analyst to verify the results and had all of our testing done before our go-live date! Howard's enterprise and resourcefulness are staggering.

Perfect Phrases for Creativity

• When approaching a problem, Hillary's first question is "What's the best way to solve it?" not "What do people usually do?" The result is innovation. For example, she streamlined part of our research process by creating and then championing the use of questionnaires for interviewing vendors and doing case studies. These are still in use by our staff today. She also injected a noticeably more international focus into her research on case studies, vendors, and the marketplace in general because she sensed our customers would value it (they do!). Hillary was also a true believer when it came to networking and our contact database. She developed a new business practice for feeding leads to our sales force that increased potential customer contacts by 12 percent. Hillary also demonstrated her innovativeness through her unwavering commitment to the three daily, bimonthly, and monthly internal publications she created and managed for us. Published on our intranet, they were read across the company and directly by the group's executive management. She also created a strategy for publicizing our wind-power research through pilot programs, submissions to online newsletters, and demonstrations. Finally, to inform her colleagues of the latest alternative energy trends, Hillary also initiated and maintained an internal daily news service on biofuels and geothermal energy.

- It's difficult for me to describe the many obstacles an investigator can encounter in achieving substantial results, but I can tell you that Tim surmounts them all with little difficulty, showing me an incredible creativity and flexibility. For instance, when he discovered that the protein produced by his plasmid was usable but could not be collected in the desired quantities, he independently taught himself advanced methods for extracting and purifying proteins and then successfully tailored and painstakingly refined these techniques to his plasmid research. This and countless other examples demonstrated to me that whenever Tim encountered a problem, he had what it takes to resourcefully use his own research skills and ingenuity to find and apply a solution. I learned early on that I never have to worry when I give Tim a lofty goal. His problem-solving confidence and independence are far above that of other would-be medical students.

- I want to emphasize Leila's natural savvy and creativity when approaching real estate projects. She has an intuitive understanding of a site's value and potential and a knack for arriving at innovative solutions to problems she's never faced before. For example, during the Palomar Mesa project, the landlord threw us two curveballs that Leila handled like a veteran. First, the landlord stipulated that we would have to acquire the entire 24,000-square-foot site, though we only needed to occupy half of it. Working with my Real Estate Director, Leila confidently and quickly signed up YourStorage to lease the rest of the property from us. Next, the landlord insisted that we and YourStorage, as the tenants, would have to pay all the expenses for converting the property—an atypical requirement. Because Leila already had excellent lease negotiation and property management experience, she came up with a masterful solution. With the landlord holding all the cards, Leila convinced YourStorage not only to share certain construction and equipment expenses but also to manage the entire property for us. Leila's skillfulness gave the landlord what it wanted, provided us with a stronger position than we had initially expected, and provided YourStorage with an equitable arrangement—a "win-win-win." I am truly impressed with Leila's instincts and creative problem solving.

- Charles is not reticent about suggesting improvements to our processes. When he joined us, our human resources department had not been keeping good track of the local laborers we hire; they were simply lumped into "overhead costs." All this data sat uncompiled in separate books of entries, and our payroll system was not integrated with the home office's. Charles told me flat out that our data management was poor and began reminding our staff that information is one of the most important things we manage. Bringing in an outside contractor, over the course of two to three months, Charles, the contractor, and our chief accountant designed a computer application dedicated solely to managing payroll data. Though not earth-shattering, this example illustrates the kind of varied impact that Charles's innovative mind has had on our organization.

• Sarah's commitment to improving the working environment of the Maritime Law Group has been significant. After she learned from colleagues that they wanted to have a formal channel through which to anonymously express their concerns to management, Sarah proposed forming a two-member Associate Committee for this purpose. Once her proposal was adopted, Sarah was elected by her associates to serve on the committee for two years. Working closely with her fellow associates, Sarah convinced the Maritime Law Group to replace our traditional "free market" assignment system, in which partners freely chose the associates they want to work with on a project. Some associates complained that under this system they could not get enough projects and were afraid they would "fall through the cracks," while others complained they sometimes received too many projects but didn't feel they could refuse a partner. Sarah organized meetings both among the associates and between the associates and partners to find a better alternative. As a result of these discussions, the Maritime Law Group adopted a new assignment system—one partner would function as the Assignment Partner to distribute projects more evenly among associates based on their needs and interests. Sarah's creativity is the reason our associates now have a system they've come to value.

Chapter 14

Perfect Phrases for Weaknesses

No section of the recommendation letter is more dreaded, mis-understood, or outright evaded than the weakness question. Most recommenders whistle past the graveyard, afraid to doom the applicant's chances by suggesting that he's imperfect. They either ignore weaknesses altogether ("If Biff has any weaknesses I am unaware of them") or dress up virtues as vices ("perfectionist," "works too hard"). Both approaches fail because they're hard to believe and too many other recommenders use them.

The purpose of the weakness question is not really to flush out the bad apples (though it can serve that purpose, too) but simply to learn where an otherwise outstanding applicant needs further development. Unless the school's question insists that you discuss a personal weakness, a much safer approach is to focus on skill-specific or professional/functional weaknesses. For credibility's sake, try to provide a brief example that illustrates the applicant's flaw, then indicate what the applicant has done to address it. If the weakness is not an egregious vice, doesn't routinely impede the applicant's effectiveness, and can be rectified, then candidly presenting it will not damage the applicant's admission chances. After all, schools are in the business of graduating new and improved versions of the imperfect people they previously admitted.

Neither you nor the applicant should fear the weakness question. A believable, concrete admission from you that the applicant is not perfect can lend credibility to the enthusiastic praise in the rest of your letter. Schools don't admit applicants because they have no blemishes. They admit them because their positives are so consistently striking and substantial as to outweigh their faults.

The examples in this chapter are divided into four categories: weaknesses involving people skills or the applicant's personality, weaknesses that are the result of immaturity or lack of experience, academic weaknesses, and weaknesses related to specific skills.

Perfect Phrases for Interpersonal or Personality Weaknesses

• Li sometimes overextends himself and commits himself to more projects than he has time for. He is, for example, deeply involved in Shìjiè Xuéxí Liánluòwǎng (SXL), a charitable organization that has taught thousands of Chinese adults how to read and write. Li told me that he had promised SXL that he would help it look for funding from international NGOs and government agencies but that because of his extremely busy work schedule he hasn't been able to follow through. Unfortunately, SXL has been left dangling as a result. I know Li is taking steps to prioritize his schedule and refuse projects he wants to work on but can't commit to. For example, he was recently offered an exciting project to establish an organization within Pacific Rim Trading that would enable us to establish new distribution markets to the millions of "mom-and-pop" shops in China that we don't reach. Although this is the kind of challenge Li normally leaps at, he turned down the offer because he knew he didn't have enough time to do it well.

• Summer has a tendency to avoid conflict or hostile situations. This is a virtue up to a point, but I know of two instances in the past year when another student has taken credit for Summer's work. I discovered only after the fact that Summer kept these incidents to herself because she believes that "justice will prevail." When she was named to the Education Department's Learning Disability Outreach Team in 2009, however, this same student was going to be placed on Summer's team. Summer immediately understood that this student's presence might have a destructive effect on the team and a cause (learning disabilities) that she cares a lot about. That's when Summer approached me and explained what the other student had done (with enough evidence to convince me she was telling the truth). My colleagues and I approached the other student with the evidence, and he confessed. He's now on academic probation from the university. I think this incident taught Summer that avoiding conflict with people who take advantage of her restraint is not in anyone's best interests.

• The only shortcoming of Michael's that I ever saw was his lack of assertiveness in large meetings. Of course, he was typically the youngest and most "junior" person in those meetings, but we value confidence, and Michael has the good judgment and insight to assert himself more confidently. I actually don't believe this trait stemmed from an absence of leadership instincts or confidence, but results from the fact that Michael was trained in the investment banking environment, where junior staff are expected to be more circumspect. With encouragement, Michael has improved, but he still has a way to go. Two years discussing cases at Harvard will bring him fully out of his shell.

• As for his weaknesses, I think Matt would admit that although he can quickly build rapport with almost anyone, he does have a tendency to take the lead role, whether it is his to take or not. At one point very early on, Matt told me to "not compromise on quality" in a way that made me feel like we were no longer peers but in a manager-employee relationship. So I told him, "You're acting like a boss to me." He wasn't expecting this, and I think it hurt him a bit. But instead of keeping his feelings bottled up, Matt and I talked about the incident. He admitted that initially he had assumed I was "just" a junior analyst and that he had not really understood my role. This immediately cleared the air, and from then on Matt treated everyone like a peer.

Perfect Phrases for Immaturity or Inexperience Weaknesses

• Cindy is a gifted sales leader, but she doesn't always make the best business decisions. This isn't a character flaw or a weakness in her potential. It's just a question of experience and training. There's a vast difference between being a sales manager, as Cindy is, and a general manager responsible for all profits and losses. For example, during a recent trip to Dubai, Cindy offered her strategy for increasing the amount of license revenue in a transaction: allow the customer to defer past-due maintenance. I pointed out that doing this would move the receivable past 120 days, thereby causing it to be classified as bad debt. This impacts the expense line, which would lower our margins for the quarter. Cindy immediately understood and changed her strategy. She understands that aside from selling and leading other salespeople, a general manager must grasp the strategic and profit-margin dimensions.

• Frank is not flawless by any means. I have seen him "gang up on" a classmate during a classroom exchange when it's clear to everyone, including Frank's classmate, that he's won his point. I don't consider this a character flaw, however. Frank is actually a warm and compassionate person. His occasional classroom "victory laps" are more about the youthful immaturity that almost all of his classmates also suffer from in one way or another. As Frank encounters peers as talented and sharp as he is at Stanford, he'll gain some humility and restraint.

• Angela has shown great potential for senior management roles at a very young age. But there are definitely areas that she should polish further to increase her chances of professional success. To this point in her career, for example, she has been primarily focused on defining product plans for specific products, but if she is to fulfill her ambitious goal of creating and managing advanced technology enterprises in Africa, she definitely needs to gain more exposure in leading larger teams. In her path toward General Manager, Angela also must learn how to build teams. Though she has led many cross-functional teams at Leapfrog Wireless and has had some experience motivating and delegating to individuals, she has had very limited experience managing direct reports. I have recommended to her that she develop her group leadership skills outside the workplace if she can, and her volunteer work coordinating tutors for Teachable Moment shows she's following my advice.

• The only thing holding Randy back from the ability to lead large organizations is a practical one: he lacks the wide professional network successful leaders rely on to gain the information and perspective to manage effectively. Though he has significant international experience, the bulk of Randy's career has been spent in Australia, and that is where his professional network is primarily based. The kind of network Randy would join as an alumnus of a school of Chicago Booth's caliber would help him develop the breadth of perspective to command the respect of everyone.

• Lucia is still relatively young given the scope of her responsibilities, and so she still possesses some youthful traits. She can be a bit naive sometimes in analyzing situations and taking people's words at face value, for example. Lucia needs to be more critical in reading between the lines and understanding the surface level of someone's words versus the reality. This is a question of experience, of course. Given Lucia's high potential, however, it would be good for her to overcome this weakness as soon as possible. Nothing would help Lucia more in this regard than law school, where the intensive group interaction will quickly confront her with her own naiveté and mistakes in reading people. She will gain maturity and "people savvy."

Perfect Phrases for Academic Weaknesses

• When Ajay began TA'ing for me, there was one area in which he really needed improvement. As he strove to explain difficult engineering concepts in class, he sometimes didn't pay enough attention to presenting ideas clearly enough so that everyone could understand them. That is, in interactions with brighter students he sometimes seemed to forget where he was and begin discussing concepts as if speaking to a fellow graduate student or faculty member. After seeing him do this a couple of times, I spoke with him about it. He is already more conscious about always translating his analysis into layman's language and ensuring that the whole class is following his train of thought.

• Lynette's intellect is as sharp as a switchblade. When she focuses it, she can analyze a problem as incisively as any student I've taught. Her weakness is her relative lack of perspective or the ability to place the problems she analyzes in a broader context. Lacking this "bigger picture"—primarily because she is still young and not widely read—she can lose the forest for the trees in her interpretations. The final result can be sophisticated linguistic exegesis but also a reading that is counterintuitive or commonsensically false. I regard this flaw as the least of Lynette's worries, however. With serious study, continual reading, and the simple passage of time, she will become as good at contextualizing issues as any of us.

• Regarding Arturo's weaknesses, I will say that in some of his papers for me he tended to try to "explain the world." He chose a subject that was too complex to handle in one thesis and then tried to force a new approach onto the whole of it, biting off much more than he could chew. I brought this up with him in my comments on his papers, and he seems to be making a better effort at limiting his focus and analyzing his subject fully.

• When Alan asked me to write a recommendation letter for him, I shared with him the one weakness I remembered from his days in my chemistry lab: a tendency in group projects to sometimes give classmates the simplest tasks when he felt he or the team would perform better if their contribution was minimized. In other words, he sometimes seemed impatient toward the collaborative process if he felt it would slow down the team's progress. Of course, building collaborative skills was one of my goals in this lab work! Because I have not seen whether Alan has developed in this area since he graduated, before writing this letter I asked him whether he was aware of this weakness and had worked on it. He admitted the problem and very candidly told me that the technical demands of research work have been so intense that he quickly learned how to rely on colleagues. I believe this weakness will not be an issue for him in medical school.

Perfect Phrases for Functional or Skill-Related Weaknesses

• The one issue I asked Damon to work on while he was in my department was his long-term planning skills. While working for me, Damon had difficulty estimating completion times for projects longer than three months. While this is a hard skill to master in a rapidly changing environment, it was the next logical step in his growth. Damon's responsibilities as Product Marketing Manager have enabled him to develop this skill, but it's something he should continue to be aware of.

• As institutional stock brokers, Jennifer and I learned how to take a research analyst's 50-page report on a company and turn it into a five-minute pitch that fits into a broader market theme within the global economy. We don't read 10-Ks, and we don't build financial models. We have more of a top-down approach to the market, in contrast to research analysts' bottom-up approach. Given Jennifer's goal of managing a mutual fund, she must learn how to understand and analyze a company from its fundamentals. Learning this skill is exactly why she and I both think the University of Wisconsin's Applied Security Analysis Program is the best place for her.

• One of the things Martin needs to work on is customer acquisition and direct sales. Up to this point in his career, he has only played a peripheral role in the entire sales process. Rising up from engineering roles, he didn't gain experience with the quotas, deadlines, and deal-closing of the direct sales role. Frankly, if Martin wants to run his own enterprise, he must understand the sales process and how to close deals. Likewise, because the products Martin has helped develop have been primarily sold as part of a larger suite, he has not had much experience in generating leads. As he gains broader responsibilities in product management, he needs to understand the process of acquiring customers and partners.

• The most important feedback I've given Takeisha is to give more thought to how she delivers her message during presentations to our investment committee. When I began working with her, I noticed that she sometimes made investment recommendations to our committee without anticipating all the types of questions and requests for additional information that our committee often throws at analysts (e.g., "What's the maximum debt load this company can take on before violating a covenant?"). Usually, Takeisha's investment approach works; her investments generate market-beating returns because she gets to know companies' business models, financial metrics, and industry environments intimately. Still, I noticed that certain committee questions could lead her off on tangents, and the committee would have to follow up with questions before giving its approval to her idea. I offered Takeisha some feedback on how to build her argument and presentation format better. We even practiced together, with me playing "investment committee." Today, Takeisha's investment recommendations are as compelling as ever, but they are now presented in a much more organized way. Above all, her recommendations are now acted on much more quickly. In fact, I can't think of a single recommendation of hers in the past year that required the committee to ask her for follow-up information.

• Bill and I both noticed many times during our entrepreneurial adventure that we lacked adequate business knowledge, even as we gained more hands-on experience. "I don't even know what I don't know!" he sometimes admitted to me. Early on, for example, we tried to think of ways to increase the sales of our corporate tax accounting services. After discussing several possible solutions, Bill purchased a business-to-business cold-calling list and prepared a script that one of our account executives could use to make cold calls. After spending thousands of dollars and expending two months' effort with poor results, someone told us we could simply outsource our lead-generation activities to a professional lead-generation company for a fraction of what we paid for the list! A simple Google search was enough to show us that we had been spending money to reinvent the wheel. We began to wonder what other mysteries of marketing we could be saving money on if we only had the right training. Bill and I both believe an M.B.A. will give him the business skills he needs much more efficiently than the trial-and-error of day-to-day business.

Part 5

Concluding Sections

Chapter 15

Perfect Phrases for Goals and Potential

Not all applicants will be expected to know exactly what they plan to do with their degrees, perhaps least of all applicants to college or law school. Medical school applicants will be expected to know only that they want to be physicians. The greatest career definition is probably expected of business school applicants—because their careers are already well under-way—and graduate school applicants—because they are seeking advanced specialization in a specific subject matter and should therefore be able to state why.

But regardless of the degree your applicant seeks, the more defined his goals are, the more mature and promising he will appear vis-à-vis competing applicants. If your applicant has described concrete and detailed goals to you, you will be doing him a disservice by failing to note these goals in the recommendation letter. Some schools specifically ask recommenders to comment on the applicant's "potential," which is another way of asking whether you believe the applicant can realistically achieve his goals. Here again, you benefit the applicant by being as specific as you possibly can about the future you see in store, including job title, industry and type of employer, and general responsibilities both 5 and 10 years down the road and longer term. Above all, avoid the clichéd "Vicki will succeed at whatever she sets her mind to."

Recommenders for an applicant to graduate school should comment on her stated research goals: Are they realistic? Original? Do they show sufficient understanding of the applicant's discipline to suggest she will successfully earn an advanced degree?

The examples in this chapter are divided into four groups: perfect phrases for business school recommenders, perfect phrases for medical school recommenders, perfect phrases for law school recommenders, and perfect phrases for college and graduate school recommenders.

Perfect Phrases for Business School Recommenders

• Robert has explained to me that he wants to eventually hold a senior leadership role in the advanced battery technology industry. Leading the productization of new battery technologies across all stages of development will be excellent preparation for his longer-term goal: a venture capital career. I believe Robert's planned path is logical, natural, and quite attainable for him. His general background in business and finance, the domain expertise in battery technology he's gained at Power Solutions, his five years of investing experience at Wells Fargo, and his master's-level understanding of electrical engineering have given him an outstanding foundation. At Power Solutions, Robert has learned the battery industry from the operational and technical level as well as the challenge of finding financing for young companies like us. To become a successful venture capitalist, however, Robert will benefit from higher-level exposure to the other challenges of start-ups in the battery technology space.

• Stan tells me his short-term post-M.B.A. goal is to work as an investment research analyst covering emerging markets either for an investment bank with a presence in Southeast Asia, such as Morgan Stanley Smith Barney, or at a mutual fund specializing in the region, such as Matthews Pacific Tiger Fund. Combined with the special insights he has gained through his working knowledge of China and Vietnam, either route will give him a rich and nuanced foundation in the market and its companies. In the long term, Stan plans to work as the fund manager of a Southeast Asia emerging markets fund. Ten to 15 years from now, I believe he will be in an excellent position to start his own fund focused on Southeast Asia or perhaps entirely on Vietnam.

• I believe Francesca will ultimately return to Mexico to start her own biotech venture. I know she believes passionately in the use of advanced gene-therapy approaches to develop drugs that cure the diseases that Mexican people are more likely to contract, such as heart disease and diabetes. She has spoken of establishing a firm that emphasizes research and development to secure a strong foothold at the high-quality, premium end of Mexico's pharmaceutical industry. If all goes according to plan, I think Francesca could then leverage strategic partnerships with global pharmaceutical companies such as GlaxoSmithKline and Sanofi-Aventis to expand her business to the U.S. and European markets in exchange for helping them increase their market share in Mexico and Central America. It's an outstanding plan, and I believe she can do it.

• Joseph has outlined for me the following career goal: performing investment banking in China and specializing in mergers and acquisitions as a corporate financial advisor. Though this goal represents a career change, the work that tax attorneys and investment bankers do shares many similarities. Both fields are project based and service oriented and require refined analytical skills. Moreover, both require an intensive familiarity with a wide range of complex business transactions. Finally, both fields require significant knowledge of the law. Joseph obviously possesses the knowledge of the law, but he has also seemed to me to be one of the most business oriented of attorneys. He already focuses on offerings of securities, particularly from Asian issuers, and on mergers and acquisitions, where he represents both buyers and sellers, both public companies and private companies. As a tax lawyer, Joseph always structures the deal, which is the most challenging and creative stage of an M&A. He also negotiates the acquisition document. In transactions with major investment banks like Barclays Capital, Goldman Sachs, and Credit Suisse, Joseph has been personally involved in everything from strategic planning to valuation and financing (all of which have important tax implications). Joseph now wants to make the switch to the other side of the table, and with an M.B.A., I see him as a leader in China's financial services industry in 10 years' time.

• Deirdre is highly motivated to succeed as manager, and in the next five years I believe she will be taking on new managerial responsibilities in British Petroleum's alternative energy operations. Evaluating alternative energy technologies for possible development, she'll have a great opportunity to recognize emerging technologies, refine her own business plan, and establish contacts in the international energy industry. Her long-term goal is to launch an alternative energy firm that will focus on sustainable but also scalable alternative energy solutions such as wind-powered desalination plants or nonsilicon-based solar power farms. With a Tuck M.B.A., I'm certain she can do it.

Perfect Phrases for Medical School Recommenders

• Because of Beth's exposure to other specializations, her volunteer work in a pediatrician's office, and her experiences with pediatrics patients this summer, I believe her main focus will remain general pediatrics. She has mentioned an interest in entering a program that assigns physicians to underserved communities after medical school before specializing in pediatrics and becoming a primary care physician. I envision her as a pediatrician in a large urban physicians group that is part of several preferred provider organization (PPO) networks and affiliated with a major hospital.

• As a gerontologist affiliated with a major urban health center in the Southeast, Davis can help treat the noncommunicable diseases that typically affect the elderly, from cancer and cardiovascular diseases to diabetes and Alzheimer's. Becoming a gerontologist—perhaps in a subscription-based "concierge" care arrangement—will enable him to provide a higher, more complex level of care to his patients; address both their primary medical care and emotional needs; and practice in a population where he can maximize his impact. I believe Davis will continue to donate his time to a free clinic like the Senior Community Clinic of El Paso, where he now volunteers weekends and holidays.

• Last year, Darrell deepened his interest in surgery through opportunities to view an appendectomy, cholecystectomy, and angioplasty as a member of Princeton University's premedical society. Learning about surgery firsthand from plastic and orthopedic surgeons as an officer of the university's surgical interest group fueled his passion for the field. He now understands better than most that surgery is a demanding profession that requires dexterity, precision, stamina, and cool but that few specialties compete with it in terms of the immediate and profound impact it can have on patients. I am sure Darrell will thrive as a surgeon.

• Because of Meredith's experience in the Harlem Hospital Center ER while completing her EMT requirement, I know she wants to spend the first part of her medical career in a city hospital. Aside from the challenging and diverse patient population, she'll have the opportunity to continue the neurological research she did at Brandeis. Ten years from now, I can picture Meredith doing part-time clinical research to help develop pharmaceuticals and pharmaceutical delivery systems or lab research in neuroscience. I think you can also count on her continuing her volunteer relationship with the

American Red Cross, not only using her Red Cross certification in disaster services but perhaps sitting on the board of directors of a local chapter, as I do. Given her roots in Wyoming, I wouldn't be surprised if Meredith devoted the latter part of her career to practicing in a rural community in her home state. It would be a natural place for her to close out her brilliant career.

• Ted has told me that his career goal is to become an outstanding clinician and ultimately join a clinical faculty where he can continue his lifelong learning while he teaches vet students what he has learned in dermatology and veterinary medicine. Ted wants to become an expert in both human and animal diseases and hopes to lecture at veterinary schools to advance veterinary science through the knowledge he gains in dermatology. Through his work with animals, he has become accustomed to dealing with the great diversity of disorders one encounters in dermatology, and he has developed an outstanding ability to determine animals' actual conditions through observation and their owners' comments. I know these skills will help Ted integrate objective findings with his clinical knowledge so he can put the "whole picture together" and gain an accurate diagnosis. Ted is bound for a distinguished career.

Perfect Phrases for Law School Recommenders

• Maureen is a bright, capable, articulate individual with that rare and valuable combination of skills required of every successful patent attorney: a facility for analyzing advanced technical and engineering problems and the capacity to lucidly and concisely explain her position in patent-related legal issues. When I first met her, I was impressed by Maureen's rationale for seeking a master's and pursuing patent examinee opportunities with the Patent and Trademark Office (PTO), and I encouraged her to join the Government Patent Lawyers Association (GPLA) and participate, network, and learn from our senior members. At subsequent GPLA events, Maureen and I had informative discussions about career opportunities with the government, patent law in general, and Supreme Court decisions and rulings on intellectual property (IP) issues. I was struck by the level of expertise and professional perspective she showed in our conversations, and her opinions on pivotal Supreme Court cases involving IP were thoughtful and articulate. Yet Maureen spoke only of patent examinee opportunities with the government and initially made no mention of an interest in a law degree. I was frankly surprised by this, given her interest in and grasp of patent law issues, and thought she might not be fully aware of the opportunities available to someone with her talent. I therefore explicitly brought up the subject of law school with her. Since then, Maureen and I have discussed professional opportunities at the PTO and in private practice for technologists with patent law degrees, and I am delighted that she is now acting on my advice. She will be an outstanding patent attorney.

• Angelo's goal is to work for shareholders' rights on a national scale, drawing on his training as a financial analyst to identify situations where minority shareholders have been abused and need a proactive advocate. Although his initial efforts with small and middle-tier corporations in Louisiana have been successful, if he intends to challenge more sophisticated corporations I know he will require a thorough immersion in the law, including the principles of fiduciary duty, securities regulation, negotiation, and, of course, litigation. After earning his J.D., Angelo will no doubt begin expanding his shareholder advocacy skills by working through an activist investment fund or by joining a conventional law firm. Whichever specific path his career takes, I'm certain Angelo will continue to fight for good corporate governance.

• Capitalizing on her exposure to tax-related issues both at Goucher College and Deery Tax Partners, after Rachel passes the Maryland bar I predict she will begin practicing estate planning as an attorney at a midsize Baltimore firm like Rowe Herteg or Lombard Street Associates. Helping clients prepare and review wills, trusts, and other related documents, Rachel will gain the expertise to ensure that clients' estate plans truly benefit their beneficiaries and that their estates will be distributed speedily, cost-effectively, and professionally.

• Trish's dream is a career in entertainment or contract law. She wants to use her unique knowledge of the recording industry from the performer's side to enlist and represent entertainment/media industry clients like her friends DJ Kid Noyze and Mos Thugg. As their agent, she will prepare and negotiate performance contracts and royalty, merchandising, licensing, distribution, and endorsement agreements, but I know she also looks forward to seeking out and structuring financing and marketing deals for them. To give herself the solid foundation to navigate the rapid changes taking place in media technologies, marketing, and finance, Trish will probably work for about five years after her J.D. in a corporate finance law environment to gain a firm understanding of corporate law basics and the Uniform Commercial Code. Trish has mentioned that her ultimate goal is to start a Miami-based boutique entertainment law firm specializing in Hispanic hip-hop artists.

• As gratifying as Lynn's volunteer work at Norby Psychological Services has been for him, I think he'll find it pales in comparison to the impact he can have as an attorney protecting patients' rights. Working initially, I imagine, for a personal injury law firm, he will learn how to defend the interests of underrepresented mentally ill patients by ensuring that psychological or psychiatric treatment receives the same insurance coverage as purely physical conditions. I wouldn't be surprised if a decade or so after his J.D., Lynn switches to the policy-making side to fight for legal parity between mental and physical ailments as a state representative, a government agency director, or a lobbyist.

Perfect Phrases for College and Graduate School Recommenders

• Given the talents I've discussed elsewhere in this letter, I believe Luke may soon be leading an R&D team in a major research university's materials engineering lab. He has the technical skills to understand and do strong research on materials foundations, and he has a long-term view about the practical applications that can be worked on. Our work together has opened a new line of research in microfabrication, which is now considered a very hot topic, and it could lead in many interesting directions in the coming years. In 10 years, Luke could be deeply involved in commercializing 3D laser microfabrication techniques and tools. Indeed, he can already design appropriate protocols and even implement them (he has already done some product development). Luke has the interest and the focus to follow up on this exciting work, so when these technologies are standardized or developed, which could be within a few years, he will be there.

• Since I first met Alice in 2006, I've known that her eventual goal was to work for an international development organization, specifically in a management role, where she can have a direct impact on developing societies. This role will enable her to follow in the footsteps of her father, who led UNICEF's South Asian efforts for many years. Today, after her extraordinary experiences in Sri Lanka with CARE, I truly believe the time is right for Alice to pursue this dream. Alice is fluent in English, Sinhala, and Tamil, which has helped us tremendously with our international clients. Though I have always thought it made sense for Alice to follow her father's lead, I understood her need to do so only after establishing her own identity with CARE. This is the best moment for her to leverage her unique background and blend of cultural and language skills and pursue management roles in an international development NGO.

• In graduate school, Brenda wants to build on the research on nutrition she did for the thesis I served as her supervisor on. Aside from continuing her lab work on nutrition, she intends to research rural nutrition patterns by examining such communities' food systems and the challenges they face in commercializing agricultural products, using pesticides, coping with hunger, providing nutrition education, and supporting farmers' markets, among other issues. She intends to examine the various stakeholders in rural nutrition for the purpose of exploring whether shared interests can be identified and then used to reach a consensus on nutrition. She will continue to explore the utility of the Q methodology—a survey technique that provides the same information as extensive interviews—as a way of verifying her qualitative research. This is a potentially rich vein of inquiry that has not been sufficiently researched in the literature. Her research plan is solid, and as her advisor I can assure you that she has the skills to bring it off.

• I believe Dean will become a minister for a nondenominational church here in Dallas such as New Shepherd Community Church or Deep Ellum Ecumenical Church. As my "apprentice" here at Plano Fellowship Church, he has expressed an interest in learning how to develop sound ministries through course work in everything from communication and church administration to biblical history. On graduating from your two-year program, he will seek a position as a full-time assistant minister in our church or a neighborhood congregation. After three to five years learning the ropes in that role, Dean will be ready to assume the responsibilities of his own congregation.

• I am not sure that Janice has found her true passion yet. In knowing her for these past two years, however, I've learned that when she discovers what she wants she is extremely goal oriented. Her drive has helped her get out of a small Kansas town and establish her potential for an educational career here at Buckley High. But I sense that while high school teaching has been a valuable experience for her, Janice feels she can have a greater impact. She has a friend and mentor who teaches at Lincoln Community College in Hartford and enjoys the challenge of teaching a somewhat older and more mature student population. I believe Janice could thrive on the faculty of an innovative community college, but she will obviously need a graduate degree to present the appropriate credentials. With one, I'm sure she'll be as inspiring and effective an instructor of college students as she has been for our high schoolers.

• I imagine Ken will want to continue investigating pollution sources in Chesapeake Bay either as a technical consultant for a research agency of the federal government or of the states of Maryland or Virginia or through a faculty position with a local university. Because he's skillful at writing the plans, applications, and grants that enabled us to obtain state and federal funding, I can envision him working with the Environmental Protection Agency to advance his interest in applying biosolids to agricultural land remediation. Whether Ken pursues a government career with a natural resources agency or an academic career will depend primarily, I'm sure, on which path will enable him to most effectively protect his beloved Bay.

Chapter 16

Perfect Phrases for Specific Degrees

Recommenders for college applicants do not need to explain why they think earning an undergraduate degree is a good idea: it goes without saying. For every other applicant, however, recommenders may want to briefly explain why they believe the degree the applicant seeks will make her goals more achievable. You should definitely consider addressing this subject if you also have the degree that the applicant is pursuing or, at least, have worked with people who do. Employers who have M.B.A.s, hire M.B.A.s, or work with M.B.A.s, for example, should be able to shed light on the benefits of a graduate management degree for the applicant. Similarly, if you earned your degree at one of the schools the applicant is targeting, you could help your applicant even more by explaining why you think she would be a great fit at your alma mater.

Perfect Phrases for Business School Recommenders

• The most constructive advice I have given Gigi is to apply to business school. She knows that Haas School of Business has had a powerful impact on my career and life. As soon as I detected Gigi's potential and ambition, I told her that the complete immersion and intense group experience of working closely with very sharp people would test her creativity and ability to think on her feet. I told her that business school will be the kind of maturing experience that will fill in her skill gaps and enable her to keep aiming high in her long-term goals. Gigi's response was very positive. She told me she has been considering earning an M.B.A. since law school because she felt it would give her the management skills to lead a law firm of her own one day. Gigi can benefit from the quantitative rigor, functional foundation, and intellectual integration that a good business school will provide.

• Last month, I discussed Tatiana's M.B.A. potential with Allen Jens (Thunderbird '00), our Vice President, whom Tatiana has approached for advice on business school. Allen bluntly said, "I wish I had sat next to someone as sharp as her when I was in business school!" I echo Allen's sentiment. Eastern Europe has no world-class business programs at all, so Tatiana must look overseas for the education she needs. Her personal research has confirmed my own feeling that UNC Kenan-Flagler's leadership emphasis and real estate resources; its small, collegial class; and its diverse, team-driven culture make it an ideal choice for her. Cypress Capital usually pays only a limited percentage of employees' M.B.A.s, but because of Tatiana's exceptional value to the company I am discussing with our VP of Human Resources the possibility of fully sponsoring Tatiana's M.B.A.

• As with other large investment banks, WestBanc reserves the Associate title for those who hold a postgraduate degree. Although Abdul currently lacks such a degree, in 2007 he was selected to attend a three-month training program in WestBanc's headquarters that was for M.B.A.s only. Moreover, as a second-year Associate, Abdul is now performing the exact same duties as an M.B.A. who has over six years of investment banking experience. Most importantly, despite lacking an M.B.A., Abdul was promoted to Associate in 2006 on the strength of his exceptional skills and performance. An M.B.A. in finance will help Abdul consolidate what he has learned and sharpen his advanced finance and managerial skills. Courses on competitive strategy; advanced financial analysis and shareholder value; and mergers, management buyouts, and other corporate reorganizations will help him round out his points of reference.

• I believe Carrie when she tells me that no other school is as strong as Columbia Business School in international development, entrepreneurship, and social enterprise—the focus of her post-M.B.A. goals. Carrie tells me she has spent the past year and a half discussing Columbia's program with its students, faculty, and alumni, and they convinced her that its innovative curriculum, Social Enterprise Program, professional clubs like the Small Business Consulting Club, and the Eugene M. Lang Center represent exactly the mix of resources her professional goals require. As a Columbia M.B.A. myself (Class of 1999), it was hard for me to disagree.

• As a Harvard M.B.A., I vividly recall the pressures of the case method, particularly during my first three months of school. But in my 11 years since business school, I've discovered that the communication skills the method taught me are more important than any technical knowledge I gained. Because Jeffrey's communication skills are polished—his sales, presentation, and negotiation skills are the best I've encountered—he will flourish in Harvard's case-based learning environment. One reason I know Jeffrey will excel at HBS is that I was the recipient of his support during my case-based technical certifications, which I took while at SAP in 2006. In this very scaled-down version of the HBS case process, Jeffrey effectively listened to my case arguments, proofread my papers, role-played with me in preparation for my board interviews, and served as a general sounding board throughout the stressful process. It says a lot about my confidence in Jeffrey that he is only the second person I've personally recommended to HBS since I earned my M.B.A. there.

Perfect Phrases for Medical School Recommenders

• One reason Ellen has chosen to pursue a career in military medicine is the broad patient population she will encounter, one that I've assured her is actually broader than physicians find in most civilian environments. I explained to her that what I've enjoyed most about military medicine is the opportunity to treat both the healthy and physically fit—in my case, Air Force personnel—as well as a broader universe of patients: the flyers' families and civilians. I've tried to help her understand that as a military physician she can experience this diversity and that it will help to prepare her for the greater diversity she will encounter if she is deployed to underserved or refugee areas overseas. Moreover, Ellen's extensive background in biotechnology will be an asset as the military copes with the special threats of bioterrorism. Ultimately, I believe Ellen is drawn to military medicine because it rewards leadership. Leadership takes many forms, and only one of them is where you sit in the chain of command.

• Troy has chosen osteopathic medicine over allopathic medicine because he believes hands-on manipulative treatment offers unique benefits in relieving pain, restoring range of motion, and enhancing the body's natural capacity to heal itself. Osteopathic medicine also promotes a stronger patient-doctor bond, and, in my experience, osteopaths are often more down-to-earth and compassionate physicians than those in other areas of specialization. Central California, where I practice and Troy has indicated he will too, is home to large, unassimilated Hmong and Mexican communities where allopathic medicine is viewed with distrust. As an osteopathic physician, Troy will be able to "infiltrate" these communities and challenge the orthodoxy that effective medicine can be provided only in a designated health facility. By working with community leaders and organizing weekend health clinics in local parks and supermarket parking lots, as I have done, Troy can help bring medicine to California's most needy.

- Patrick confessed to me that during his mission trips to Sierra Leone, he was shocked to learn that 90 percent of the cases were children with easily curable ailments like malnutrition, lice, and fungal cases. That's when his interest in pediatrics began. When I first got to know Patrick, he told me that he believed that the best way for him to serve was as a primary care pediatrician with a free clinic in a poor part of the United States. I responded that while pediatricians are always definitely needed, in many regions of the world general surgeons are even more valuable because their internal medicine and surgery skills make them so versatile. Since that conversation and Patrick's shadowing experiences with me, he's shifted his career focus options to surgery. A medical degree will enable him to realize his goal of running a low-fee surgical clinic modeled after my hospital's Mercy Center where he will practice general or orthopedic surgery.

Perfect Phrases for Law School Recommenders

- Last summer, Eileen's father convinced me to offer her a clerkship here at Berrigan Stansfield & Wood so she could see how law is practiced "out West." I think we made a big impression on her. I assigned her to help two of our attorneys escort a major Colorado corporation through the state and federal permitting processes so it could expand its manufacturing facility in an area identified by environmentalists as threatened. Eileen was obviously fascinated by the origins and intricacies of landmark environmental acts like the Clean Water Act and Toxic Substances Control Act and peppered me with questions about the delicate balance between businesses' right to exploit natural resources and environmentalists' right to protect them. Her research into Colorado regulatory law actually helped our client prevail in an administrative hearing seeking relief from an overburdensome EPA regulation. Eileen clearly loved her time here in Boulder, so much so that she now wants to earn her J.D. at the University of Colorado at Boulder because of its rich resources in environmental law, from the Natural Resources Law Center to the Natural Resources Litigation Clinic.

• Although Dylan majored in accounting at Stanford, out of curiosity in his senior year he took my business law elective, in which we discussed the U.S. Bankruptcy Code (Title 11) and famous tort-related bankruptcies like Johns-Manville, Dow Corning, and Texaco. He wrote a paper for me on the early history of composition agreements that was superb. When I half-jokingly asked him whether he'd ever considered law school, he spent the next 15 minutes telling me how much he'd enjoyed my class and what extra reading around the law he'd been doing. I invited him to test his interest by helping on the research for my history of bankruptcy law in Yolo County. He passed the test. Like me, he's attracted to the mix of litigation and transaction work that bankruptcy law entails and the range of law it touches, from tax issues and contracts to loans and leases. Dylan's plan during law school is to clerk for a summer with a major bankruptcy boutique firm such as Friedman Dumas &

Springwater or McNutt & Litteneker. After law school, I've encouraged him to clerk for a bankruptcy judge so he can understand bankruptcy law through a judge's eyes. After his law degree, my guess is that Dylan will pursue a solo practice representing secured creditors like insurance companies and banks in Chapter 11 cases.

• Because Boston is where Kristy intends to practice, she is applying to Boston College, Boston University, and Northeastern University. All are fine schools, of course, with many of the resources she needs, but Kristy and I agree that Boston College is head and shoulders above its peers in the areas that matter most to her: range of clinical programs, writing classes, and overseas opportunities (such as the Holocaust/Human Rights Project and International Criminal Tribunal). Kristy has also mentioned to me that as a practicing Catholic, BC's Jesuit tradition matters a lot to her. It's a match made in heaven.

Perfect Phrases for Graduate School Recommenders

• Almost from the minute we met, Alphonso was telling me that he planned to pursue his master's in engineering in the United States. He said America had the world's best computer engineering programs, and his dream was to become a programmer in Silicon Valley. He told me he had experienced the dynamism of American business as a teenager visiting relatives in Miami and was always told by his father that in an age of global markets if you don't have an international degree it can be tough to succeed. During lunch hours, I would sometimes see Alphonso researching the programs and specialties of U.S. engineering schools on the Web, and I was also surprised to learn that he seemed to read only English-language books. When I asked him why, he said, "To improve my English for America." After rising to lead programmer, Alphonso intends to establish a company of his own. I was not surprised to learn that his number-one choice for graduate school was Stanford.

• A Ph.D. is essential to Kim's goal of teaching at the university level and pursuing research at the intersection of sleep and immunology. As an undergraduate summer student at the University of Nebraska Center for Sleep and Chronobiology, she became intrigued by the fact that patients who are sleep-deprived often complain not only of tiredness and fatigue but also of frequent colds and flus. Suspecting there may be a link between the immune system and sleep, she began the research she's continued under my direction into the neural actions of substances that are both immune-enhancing and sleep-inducing. Through graduate-level courses and labwork, Kim will deepen her understanding of the link between sleep and immunology. A cross-disciplinary doctoral program like the University of Minnesota's will also enable Kim to explore the ethical and social dimensions of her research. For example, many patients with debilitating mental conditions like chronic fatigue syndrome are stigmatized and denied medical benefits because the causes of their conditions are unknown. A cutting-edge Ph.D. program like Minnesota's Immunology and Sleep Medicine program will enable Kim to uncover the underlying pathologies of these mental health–related diseases.

Chapter 17

Perfect Phrases for Conclusions

The purpose of an effective conclusion is simple: to make a final ringing endorsement of the applicant's candidacy, rounding out the sustained tone of enthusiasm that has characterized your entire letter. Avoid tired or pro forma conclusions that smack of insincerity or indifference: try to close with some detail or sentiment that captures what makes *this* applicant so special.

Note that many of the following examples specifically name the applicant's target school because recommendation letters that are tailored to the applicant's target school are usually better than generic letters. For many applicants and recommenders, of course, a school-specific letter won't be feasible.

• Lian deserves a place in Stanford's Class of 2012 because she has demonstrated repeatedly and impressively that she has the skills that turn promising ideas into revolutionary technologies. I

187

wish her the best of luck. Should you wish to discuss this reference in more detail, please feel free to call me at (123) 456-7890.

- If he chose to, Richard could build an outstanding, even singular career for himself as a scholar of Brazilian history. Indeed, I have urged him more than once to seriously reconsider abandoning his Ph.D. work. But the reasons Richard gave me for wanting to pursue a law degree were so thoughtful, concrete, and persuasive that I eventually stopped trying. Though the contribution he could make to history would be substantial, he will likely make just as significant an impact in the law. I say that not because I am an expert in the law, but because I have recommended three students to Yale Law School who eventually earned J.D.s there, and Richard's intellectual and language skills are at least as strong as theirs. He is without question among the top 1 percent of students I have worked with in my 25-year career. Feel free to contact me at the phone number or e-mail below if I can provide any more information about Richard Montacci.

- I am pleased to provide Jack Sims with my highest recommendation. He will be an asset to Wharton as he has been for us. I would be delighted if I could work with Jack again in the future.

- We recommend Fang to Oregon Health and Science University's admissions committee with enthusiasm and confidence. We urge you to accept her application and assure you she will thrive in medical school as she has here at Swarthmore.

- Thomas is on the fast track for quick promotion and development as a senior underwriter. I would love to have him here at

Transamerica for another year, but given his career goals I believe it would be a poor use of his professional development time. He needs and deserves the challenge that Duke's M.B.A. program can provide. I give him my unqualified endorsement.

- When I learned a young officer was being assigned as our Assistant Gunnery Officer, I couldn't help but think that planning for a war was going to be hard enough without having to train a young commander with no battle experience. Little did I know that Antonne's contribution would play such a large role in the mission success of our vessel. Antonne's departure from the Navy is a great loss. He is already missed, but he left his mark, and his leadership is being carried forward by the sailors he led and trained. I'm honored to have served with him and strongly urge you to accept his application to your education program. Antonne will make an outstanding teacher.

- I've worked with many students over the course of my career, and I find Jodi to be truly special. She possesses a rare combination of analytical rigor, gracefully incisive writing skills, and original scholarly ideas. I look forward to witnessing the impact she will have in the years ahead. There is nothing she cannot do.

- I have advised four students who ultimately graduated from Vanderbilt's Peabody College of Education and Human Development, and Bruce's ability and potential compare favorably with them. He has shown the potential to be a truly outstanding educator and will be a credit to your program. I wish him every success in his teaching career.

- In closing, I would like to emphasize that Boston Consulting Group has decided to finance Ms. Treadwell's M.B.A. study at NYU Stern and is eager to reemploy her as a consultant when she completes the program. This reflects the very high esteem we have for her.

- Thank you for considering Deepak's application. He has every qualification to join his grandfather, father, and eldest sister as a future member of Amherst College's proud alumni association.

- Christina Koo's potential, both professionally and personally, is unlimited. As an applicant to Tuck, she is the "complete package"; I cannot recommend her strongly enough.

- Elsa has greatly enriched my chair, our department, and our institution as a whole. I'm certain she has a successful, even illustrious, academic career before her. Both professionally and personally, I strongly support Elsa Robbins's application for admission to California Institute of Technology's Aeronautics program.

- In sum, George has the self-discipline, determination, problem-solving, and academic abilities to succeed in a rigorous medical curriculum and career. I endorse his decision to dedicate himself to dermatology without qualification or reservation. He is the kind of physician I would trust with my own care.

- Whether he is focusing on softball or satellites, Christopher excels as a team member and leader. He has encouraged all those around him to exceed expectations and supported them in every way he could. This has been his pattern since I first met him three years ago, and I know it will be his pattern as he pursues his M.B.A. at Kellogg.

• I have nothing but high praise for Beth's abilities and potential. I know she plans a career in patent law/intellectual property with the PTO or a private firm. I also know she is interested in pursuing the international dimension of intellectual property work, including technology transfer and global patent rights issues. Whichever area of patent law Beth ultimately chooses, her tenure at the PTO will be an unbeatable advantage for her. She has the educational background and technical expertise, the personality, and the raw talent to be a star in this profession. With a rigorous, focused legal education at George Washington University, she can go as far as she chooses. I recommend Beth Dandridge to you in the strongest possible terms. Please call me if you have any questions whatsoever.

• Your favorable consideration of Ling's application will be greatly appreciated not only by myself but by all the teachers and classmates at Ben Franklin High who have come to admire her heart and courage these past four years. She will reap rich rewards from Goshen College's internationally oriented program and will certainly become a long-term credit to your institution.

• I don't recommend individuals to the world's best business schools often or do it lightly. Moreover, I know that a recommendation only has value if it is a candid, objective statement. It is in that light that I assure you that Azool has the talent, values, and dedication to make a memorable impression on the Washington Olin community. I recommend him to you with absolute conviction.

• By overcoming her personal challenges, Janet has shown herself to be not only a very rare individual but an extraordinary scientist with an incredibly bright career ahead of her. I speak for the entire chemistry faculty at the University of Tennessee in exhorting you to admit her to your medical program. We certainly all regard Janet as a logical candidate for your Weedman Scholarship program.

• I can't think of anyone more poised to flourish in the rigorous intellectual climate of Oxford's divinity studies program than Travis Small. I urge you to give his application your favorable consideration.

• I am saddened at the possibility of losing Norm to business school next fall. However, I realize how much he will gain from Texas McCombs, so I wish him the best. I hope he will choose to return to Ball Corp. after his studies, as he will be even more of an asset than he is today.

• In my experience, gifted young people like Shaquille are few and far between. My fellow Broadman Prep teachers and I would greatly appreciate a favorable final decision on his application to Dickinson. Should you need any further information in your deliberations, my direct phone is (123) 456-7890.

• I was pleased that Josh asked me to recommend him to Wisconsin's Master in Education program; I can do so with sincere confidence. He is the kind of individual the teaching profession desperately needs more of. I'm happy to support Josh Pate's application in any way I can.

- I have thoroughly enjoyed teaching Paul. All of the history faculty at Texas Tech were openly disappointed when they learned that Paul had decided to pursue law school rather than a doctorate here. Our loss is surely your gain.

- I will close with this flat endorsement: I consider Mr. Jimenez to be an outstandingly strong candidate for admission to any medical school in the country. He is bound for great things.

- I am glad that Ms. Miyagi attended Walnut Hills High School. Hers is the classic story of a young Asian student who came here to pursue her American dream and contribute to her new society. She has done both with great success, and I am happy to have taught and advised her during the crowning two years of her high school career. I'm very, very impressed with Maho and always will be. She belongs at Princeton University.

- I'm certain that Randy merits a place at Vanderbilt Law School. I can think of no higher way to demonstrate my esteem for him than to admit that I have already extended him an offer to join Mitsubishi Heavy Industries as in-house counsel after he earns his J.D.

- I can't imagine a person I'd rather have as a student or colleague than Jason Blank. He is poised to have a tremendous impact on the scientists he chooses to research with and on geophysics as a discipline.

About the Author

Paul S. Bodine is the author of *Great Application Essays for Business School, Great Personal Statements for Law School, Perfect Phrases for Business School Acceptance, Perfect Phrases for Law School Acceptance*, and *Perfect Phrases for Medical School Acceptance*. One of America's most experienced admissions consultants (serving clients since 1997), his clients have earned admission to such elite universities as Harvard, Yale, Stanford, University of Chicago, Columbia, Dartmouth, UC Berkeley, Northwestern, University of Pennsylvania, MIT, Michigan, Virginia, Duke, and Cornell, among many, many others worldwide. A graduate of the University of Chicago and Johns Hopkins University, he lives in Southern California.

The Right Phrase for Every Situation...Every Time

Perfect Phrases for Building Strong Teams
Perfect Phrases for Business Letters
Perfect Phrases for Business Proposals and Business Plans
Perfect Phrases for Business School Acceptance
Perfect Phrases for College Application Essays
Perfect Phrases for Cover Letters
Perfect Phrases for Customer Service
Perfect Phrases for Dealing with Difficult People
Perfect Phrases for Dealing with Difficult Situations at Work
Perfect Phrases for Documenting Employee Performance Problems
Perfect Phrases for Executive Presentations
Perfect Phrases for Landlords and Property Managers
Perfect Phrases for Law School Acceptance
Perfect Phrases for Lead Generation
Perfect Phrases for Managers and Supervisors
Perfect Phrases for Managing Your Small Business
Perfect Phrases for Medical School Acceptance
Perfect Phrases for Meetings
Perfect Phrases for Motivating and Rewarding Employees
Perfect Phrases for Negotiating Salary & Job Offers
Perfect Phrases for Perfect Hiring
Perfect Phrases for the Perfect Interview
Perfect Phrases for Performance Reviews
Perfect Phrases for Real Estate Agents & Brokers
Perfect Phrases for Resumes
Perfect Phrases for Sales and Marketing Copy
Perfect Phrases for the Sales Call
Perfect Phrases for Setting Performance Goals
Perfect Phrases for Small Business Owners
Perfect Phrases for the TOEFL Speaking and Writing Sections
Perfect Phrases for Writing Grant Proposals
Perfect Phrases in American Sign Language for Beginners
Perfect Phrases in French for Confident Travel
Perfect Phrases in German for Confident Travel
Perfect Phrases in Italian for Confident Travel
Perfect Phrases in Spanish for Confident Travel to Mexico
Perfect Phrases in Spanish for Construction
Perfect Phrases in Spanish for Gardening and Landscaping
Perfect Phrases in Spanish for Household Maintenance and Child Care
Perfect Phrases in Spanish for Restaurant and Hotel Industries

Visit mhprofessional.com/perfectphrases for a complete product listing.

Learn more. Mc Graw Hill Do more.